To Pa

OTHER WORKS BY JC GARDNER

HEATED

JC Gardner

PERFECT PUBLISHING
Washington, DC

www.perfectpublishing.com

Copyright © JC Gardner, 2017

PUBLISHER'S NOTE

This is a book of fiction. Names, characters, places, and incidents are either the product of author's imagination or are used fictitiously. Any resemblance to actual persons, living or dead, business establishments, government agencies, events or locales is entirely coincidental.

International Standard Book Number
ISBN-13: 978-1-942688-42-6
ISBN-10: 1942688426

Printed in the United States of America.

Dedication
For Katrina Amy

JERILYN

CHAPTER 1

I *needed* to land this job. I smoothed out my secondhand designer suit and adjusted the safety pin holding the waistline together. The button was hanging from a thread at the time of purchase, much like I was. I just never got around to fixing it.

My eleven-year-old son, DeMarcus, was off his meds again, so he was running around the house wound up like an out-of-control spinning top, pickin' at his little sisters who had a different daddy than him.

DeMarcus' daddy didn't believe in ADHD. He said DeMarcus didn't have nothin' a good butt whuppin' couldn't cure. So as usual, I was left with the side effects after his once-a-month, weeklong court ordered visitation with his father, his live-in girlfriend, and her two delinquent teenagers.

My two younger children, fraternal twins, dove into their pop-up tent. They knew he wouldn't follow them in there. His fear of tight spaces kept them safe. He stomped his feet at their *disappearance* and started turning around in a circle.

Last time, he spun himself nauseous and threw up on my used, *brand new* sofa.

I approached him gingerly. Yelling and screaming at him only escalated the problem. I gently stopped him. "DeMarcus, please don't do this."

He snatched away from me, like how dare I touch him, and he addressed me like he was in charge. "Jerilyn, you see I'm spinnin'!"

His flagrant lack of disrespect stunned me, but I was walking a thin line and had to weigh my words and put my foot down at the same time.

"Please don't call me that. I'm your mother and you gonna respect me."

He kept spinning, singing "La, la, la" trying to drown me out.

I was mentally and physically beat. I didn't know how much longer I'd be able to handle him off his meds. He was stocky and growing every day; we already met eye-to-eye at five-foot-five.

I often wondered if this was a ploy by his father, Antoine, to eventually gain full custody of him, knowing that one day DeMarcus would go bonkers and there wouldn't be anything I could do about it. Just another battle for me in my long list of trials and tribulations.

Of course, he would then be able to claim DeMarcus for social services. It was all about him getting that paper.

I approached DeMarcus. "I have something for you." I placed the pills and a glass of water in DeMarcus' hands.

He threw the pills to the ground and shoved the water back at me.

"My daddy says I don't need that stuff. It's poison."

When he was like this, I'd learned to give him water, along with other light-colored drinks in a paper cup so the damage to the floor, sometimes the wall, was minimal. I had cleaned the carpet until it was raw from his rants and ended up ripping it up in spots. Probably will cost me my security deposit in the long run. I picked up the pills and trashed them.

Now he was flying like an airplane, arms outstretched wide like eagle's wings. I repeated the process, holding a tight grip on my internal fury, because I wanted to scream.

"Please take your medication. If not, you'll have to sleep in the dark tonight."

He stopped and blinked a few times. "So? I'm not afraid of the dark no more. Daddy says that's for sissies. I'm no sissy."

I wasn't prepared for that comeback. The fear of the dark was my number one threat that usually worked with him, and now Antoine had taken it away from me. I shook my head and turned on my heels into the kitchen while DeMarcus found the remote and flipped mindlessly through the cable stations – over eight hundred channels. We only had cable because my last boyfriend spliced it from the outside, tapping into my neighbor's connection upstairs and then hooked ours up to a "hot" box. I figured I'd ride that train until it stopped.

I crushed the pills finely and put them into some lemonade, his favorite drink *this* month. I observed him from the kitchen as he settled on a rap music channel, something else he'd picked up from his daddy.

I asked the Lord for strength while returning to the combination living room, dining room and handed him a cup of lemonade. "DeMarcus, here's some lemonade for you, your favorite."

He was in a zone and reached for the cup and drank it down at once; he licked his lips and scrunched up his face. "Tastes funny."

I chose not to comment and trashed his cup while he recited Lil Wayne lyrics like he wrote them. My two daughters, age seven, were engrossed in putting puzzles together. Me and their daddy dated for three months and they were the result of one night of no protection. We broke up before they arrived. He was now married and in the service. We got a check every month and that was about it. They were fiercely protective of each other and created an inner circle of just the two of them.

DeMarcus made them that way.

I loved my son so much. He was a smart, funny guy. Usually helpful too. But that was after consistent use of his prescribed meds. He needed them every day and it took a while to get him back on track. By then, though, he was back with his dad, and the vicious cycle would start again. His stupid-ass father refused to get with the program because of some backwoods mentality that Black folks don't need medication and they don't get ADHD. *It's just another ploy by the white* man *to keep us down. First cocaine, then heroin, now Rit'lin. Same shit*, according to Antoine.

But apparently weed did not fit into this category, and Antoine used it liberally.

This windmill effect of my son being on and off of his medication caused him to be placed in Special Ed classes. My son should have been in the sixth grade but he was in the fifth. I tried to explain all of this to Antoine, but it was a waste of time. *The boy's a little slow, that's all.*

I contemplated letting DeMarcus stay there for a month with no meds. Then perhaps Antoine would see exactly what I was talking about. I always erased those insane thoughts. Among other things, my biggest fear was that my son would be dead after Antoine tried to beat a cure into him.

No, there had to be a better way. Once I got myself together, I planned to talk with legal aid about my rights and doing what's best for my son.

DeMarcus and I resembled each other. We were both caramel colored, with coarse, thick hair. I loc'd my hair three years ago, which was the best thing I could have ever done. It was low maintenance and easy to style. We both had the same full lips and opal eyes. His nose was broad like his father's; mine was narrower. I wanted to loc his hair too but again, his sperm donor objected, saying we weren't Jamaicans. Just thinking about Antoine's ignorant ass made me question my own decision-making process, especially with men.

I really didn't think I looked all that remarkable, but I knew how to fix myself up for a night on the town; or in this case, for a job interview.

Lord, if I had only kept my legs closed instead of being wooed by Antoine's big dreams and broken promises. At the time, I was twenty-four and still into the club scene. That was my weekend fix. And that's where I met Antoine. I knew he was from the streets but I didn't know how deep the streets were *in him*. He had so much promise – *he was gonna quit hustlin' and get a real job; he was gonna get his G.E.D.; he was gonna be a businessman.* It didn't help that he was six-foot-two of toned muscles, had smooth skin the color of deep chestnut, with chocolate eyes and a goatee. He had swag and an easy way about him. In our early days of dating, he'd make me laugh out loud with his keen sense of humor. But shit changed up real quick when I realized I was the one doing all the giving. And boy, did I pay for my generosity.

CHAPTER 2

He and his boy, Kinnard, wanted to open up a used car business. Naturally, they didn't have the capital to pull it off. At the time, I was working full-time as a secretary for an insurance company. It was my first job after I got my Associates Degree in office management. I was there four years and would probably still be there if my old boss, Mr. Shaunessey, didn't die of a sudden heart attack. His wife promptly sold the business, and I was out of a job.

Antoine and Kinnard worked at Ben's Liquor Store and also sold weed on the side. Somehow, they managed to save up three thousand dollars but didn't have a lick of credit.

My dumb-ass cosigned a loan for them to get a fleet of starter vehicles. Six months into the business, unbeknownst to me, these fools torched the lot to collect the insurance money.

The only problem with that was the druggie they hired to do their dirty deed couldn't keep his mouth shut and every time they turned around he wanted money – big money. So he blabbed! Needless to say, there was no payout of insurance money. The loan for the vehicles became payable, and it was a hot mess. Antoine and Kinnard took a plea deal and did minimal jail time. I was left holding the bag, looking like boo-boo the fool! I didn't know I could hate anyone until I had to file bankruptcy.

With all of the stress I was under, I had lost track of my cycle and next thing you know, here comes DeMarcus. By the time DeMarcus was born, me and Antoine were more than on the outs. After all he put me through, that nut actually thought I was going to be sitting at home waiting for his release. Hell to the no! When he found out I was pregnant, he told me wasn't nothing going to keep him away from his son; he wasn't going to be an absentee father like his dad was. Well, he was already following in his father's footsteps by taking up residence in prison, so his words meant little to nothing to me. But sure 'nuff when he got released, he showed up a few days later demanding visitation rights. His sister helped him file paperwork to make it legal, and I haven't been able to shake him ever since.

Antoine did not pay child support. That was one deal we made that he followed through on. Instead, he would buy all of DeMarcus' clothes and must-have gadgets. I don't know how, but the boy's closet stayed packed with the latest gear. It seemed every other month, my son came home with a new pair of designer sneakers. DeMarcus had an X-Box, a Playstation, and an iPhone – all supposedly *purchased* by Antoine working at the cut-rate liquor store part-time.

I glanced at the clock and cursed under my breath. I couldn't afford to be late for this interview. *Where was she?*

No sooner did I have that thought, I was opening to the knock on the door, letting her in.

CHAPTER 3

I went to hug her, but she dodged my affection. "Thank God! I didn't think you were coming."

"Did I have a choice?" My sister, Carmella, marched in, still dressed in her hospital scrubs, having worked a double shift as a nurse's assistant at the Washington DC Veterans Medical Center.

Carmella closely resembled our father, with light skin and a spattering of freckles on both cheeks. Her hair was long and thin, as was her frame. The joke was since I was older, I stole her curves and she got the leftovers. If I could, I'd gladly give her an extra portion of breasts and hips. She took our daddy's height, at a little over five-eight, and also his temperament.

My sister was so pretty to me, but right now, she was a teapot about to go off!

She took one look at DeMarcus rocking back and forth on the couch and freaked out.

"Oh hell naw! Is this boy off his meds?"

I tried to remain calm, while the hairs on the back of my neck began to rise. I breathed deeply, suddenly aware of the nerve endings under my skin. I willed them to be still and within seconds, the feeling was gone.

I spoke soft but sternly. "Can you lower your voice? I don't want him to hear you."

"What? I don't give a rat's ass about what he hears. Is this boy off his meds or not!?" She was still loud, hands on hips, clearly distressed.

I tried to overlook her attitude. I checked my bag, making sure I had an extra copy of my resume handy, tissues and my compact.

"He was with his daddy and you know how that goes."

She cocked her neck. "I know how *that* goes? I don't know shit! I never understood why you hooked up with his triflin' ass in the first place. And you know I can't watch this boy like this, I swear!" And she continued talking aloud to herself as my eyes followed her and she went down the hall to the bathroom opening and closing the vanity cabinet, then the medicine cabinet; then she came to the kitchen on some scavenger hunt, looking for God knows what.

I finally asked, exasperated, "What're you looking for?"

"Some Nyquil."

"You sick?"

"It's for that boy! His ass needs to go to sleep! I knew I should-a just told you 'no'. This is just ridiculous! I ain't even getting paid! Look at him, rockin' like he is in some damn battery operated rocking chair about to blast off! This just ain't right, Jerilyn!" She was fuming.

I glanced at my watch, not sure at this point how I was

going to arrive on time. I was almost in tears. If she left, I was up the creek, and it seemed I'd been up there most of my life.

School had just ended and there was always this awkward week of finding daycare between summer break and the beginning of camp. It wasn't so much of a problem right now because I didn't have a job.

I grabbed my purse. "Look, I took care of him, okay. He'll calm down soon. Charisse and Courtney are in the tent, probably asleep, and you know I don't have nobody else to call."

"Why don't you call *your* mama next time? Maybe she can watch these kids. Oh yeah, that's right. They don't have childcare in prison."

CHAPTER 4

That stung me in my heart like porcupine needles shot from a bow like arrows. *Our* mother was locked up for killing our cheating father. Shot him several times in front of his lover while the white woman just screamed like a banshee in the corner. She tried to fire the gun at her too, but ran out of bullets.

Carmella disowned her, unforgiving of the fact we had to go and live for five years with our strict and at that time, newly converted Jehovah's Witnesses grandparents, after being raised Baptist. Well it was three years for me because the day after I turned eighteen, I moved in with my twenty-four-year-old cousin, Danita, who was in medical school on a full scholarship. She had her own two-bedroom condo in D.C. near Logan Circle, a BMW, and a steady paycheck from being a high-paid exotic dancer and a bartender. She also did private parties. She knew our situation, so allowing me to move in, as she put it, *was the least she could do*. I stayed with Danita two years and finished college. She taught me how to drive and cook and she was a neat fanatic, so I learned how to keep a place clean. Once Danita became a doctor, she sold her condo and moved to California. She even asked me did I want to come. I should've gone with her, but leaving Carmella behind was not an option. I miss her a lot and one day when I get the money, that's going to be my first plane ride.

Carmella was three years younger, so she had to stay with our grandparents. I would get her most weekends and every Sunday night was a huge fight not to go back, but they had legal custody. I was in no position to take care of her. The day after she turned eighteen, she left as well – and moved in with her jive-ass boyfriend, Jamal. That's another story.

Because of this, Carmella had a lot of pent-up bitterness against our mother and she blamed her for everything, even things that were not her fault. Carmella resented our new religious lifestyle, even though me and Danita did everything to make it up to her by celebrating things like birthdays and Christmas outside the home. I also made it my business to go see Mama once a month; I always had to find someone else to watch the kids during that time because I couldn't waste Carmella's time with *that nonsense*.

Our grandparents were good to us. Other than our religious differences, we wanted for nothing, but Carmella would never admit that. She lived in the past and kept her distance from them. On the other hand, I called them once a week, but I hadn't seen them in two years since they moved south.

So Lucille Bateman was always *my* mother. I swallowed hard. I wanted to respond to Carmella's nasty-ass comment, but I didn't have time for a knock-down, drag-out argument.

Carmella saw the pain she caused. She blew a long sigh. "Go on and get outta here and get that job so you can get you a real sitter." She held the door open for me.

I quickly headed for the elevator and pressed the *down* button. The light flickered like a flawed firefly; then it went out. After a few seconds, I pressed it again. I didn't have time for this.

As I stood there waiting, something felt off. Damn!! I searched my purse and quickly headed back to my apartment, where Carmella greeted me at the door.

"Guess you'll be needin' these." I grabbed her car keys dangling from her fingers and used the staircase.

• • •

I sat in her dated Honda Accord that looked like a burglarized trailer home and leaned back against the headrest praying for a break, a reprieve, something – whatever He required to get me over this hump. For twelve months at the local community college, I had been working temporarily as a file clerk, but doing executive assistant duties. That way, they didn't have to pay the temp agency a higher fee. But it was a job. I just knew they were going to hire me permanently. Instead, I was let go with one day's notice – something about a restructuring, but the only *restructure* that occurred seemed to be eliminating my position.

I took out my cosmetic pouch to adjust my look when a bead of sweat formed on my upper lip and my arms tingled like mini electric shocks, traveling down into my fingertips. I gripped the steering wheel while the heat rose up in me from the Arabian Desert. I breathed deeply as the sweat slid down the side of my face, leaving a streak in my makeup. Those few seconds of purgatory left me in tears, emotionally upset that the end of one cycle of life began another cycle of physical torment. It eventually passed, leaving me clammy and wet. I dabbed my face dry, picking off the tissue lint that was left behind.

I put the car in gear and after three blocks, the empty gas warning signal started chiming. There was no way I could stop for gas; I pushed the envelope and went over the speed limit for twenty minutes, heading down to the prestigious public relations firm of Steinway, Connolly and Birch located in Farragut Square.

My intent was to find on-the-street parking to save money, but I had only minutes to spare and was forced to pull into a private garage. I shut the car off and said a short prayer.

"Father in heaven. Please help me get this job. I need it really bad. And as always, please keep my lips in check! Thank you Jesus."

And I ran to the interview.

CHAPTER 5

Security in the building was tight. I sat in a waiting room nervous as hell with what appeared to be a few other candidates or guests. I was the only woman. We were all awaiting an escort to our final destinations, but I noticed I was the only one glancing at my watch. Repeatedly.

A portly woman with ivory skin and a pixie haircut approached me. "Ms. Bateman, please follow me."

I smoothed out my clothing and followed her to another floor. She led me to a receptionist area.

I noticed the offices were tastefully decorated in deep purple and gray. Fresh flowers graced two end tables. A leather sofa and two upholstered chairs provided ample seating. A small coffee table offered various magazines, none of which I could focus on. The receptionist's name plate read: "Porter Grant." He was well dressed in a black Stacy Adams pinstriped suit. A plum colored shirt popped from under his jacket. His hair was close shaven and his chocolate skin was smooth and flawless. His designer glasses were thin wireframes which illuminated his hazel eyes.

She introduced us, and I reminded myself to turn off the "hood" and put on the "good."

I flashed my brightest smile, having inherited my mother's perfect set of teeth. "Hi there. I'm Jerilyn Bateman. I'm here to see Miss Steinway."

He glanced at his watch. "Yes, you had a two o'clock appointment, is that correct?"

Damn, I was only eight minutes late but being kept in that other room actually delayed me even more. I kept an upbeat attitude. "Yes, that is correct. Parking was quite a challenge."

"Do you have an updated resume?" Porter had a slight Southern accent and a small gap between his two front teeth.

"Yes, of course." I passed him my resume. "Actually, nothing has changed though."

"No problem." He smelled so nice…Eternity for men. I found him quite attractive. Clearly I had been missing some serious loving for quite a while. I hovered over his desk just a hair too long.

He looked up at me. "Did you need something, Miss Bateman?"

"Uh, no. I'm good. Well, actually, where are you from? I detect a slight accent."

He smiled. "I'm from Louisiana by way of Katrina."

"What? You were there during that terrible hurricane?"

He nodded. "Yes. I lost everything. I moved here to D.C. to live with my older brother till things got better. I thought I'd be gone by now, but I landed this great job working for Miss Steinway."

I wondered how somebody who lost everything could afford designer suits, but since we didn't know each other like that, I couldn't dare begin to find out. Not yet anyway.

I kept the conversation going. "Ms. Steinway. That's who I would be working for too, right?"

He raised an eyebrow. "Well, yes, I guess so."

"Where would I sit?"

"If you were to get the position, you'd be sitting right there." He pointed to another work station a few feet from him that I had not noticed. He got up and disappeared into the office in back of him, then returned shortly afterwards.

I walked over to the workstation that looked like it was being used as spare storage space. I walked around the desk trying to evoke good karma over it that this spot could only be for me. I quietly recited my own versions of scripture....*No weapon formed against me shall prosper or occupy this desk; if this desk is for me, who can be against me; all things work together for the good who love the Lord...and need a job.*

His phone rang and after a brief conversation, he said, "Ms. Steinway will see you now."

"Do you have any advice for me?"

"Just be you."

CHAPTER 6

Ms. Steinway was an older white woman with stark white hair tightly pulled off of her face into a bun. Her blue eyes peered at me over her red-framed reading glasses.

She was standing up in a dark blue Anne Klein suit, sheer hose, and conservative pumps. Authentic pearls adorned her neck and ears. She extended her hand. "Ms. Bateman."

I shook her hand, which had a firm grip. "Nice to meet you, Ms. Steinway, and I'm really excited about being considered for this Project Assistant position."

"Please, have a seat." The rings on her left hand were sparkling, an estimated four carats.

She sat down, crossed her legs and removed her glasses. "Ms. Bateman, I'm afraid I owe you an apology. This is a bit awkward and definitely out of the ordinary. Actually, it is quite embarrassing."

She let out a distressing sigh. "There is no easy way to say this, but the job has been filled. There was simply not enough time to reach you and, well, things happened so fast. I really am sorry."

I blinked as if that would change what I heard. I leaned forward, "Excuse me? Can you repeat what you just said?"

"I'm really sorry, Ms. Bateman. Again, my apologies." She stood up. "If something else opens up, we'll be in touch." She extended her hand.

Pissed did not adequately explain how I was feeling. I should have just gracefully left the building, but I couldn't, and before I knew it, my mouth was at the starting line and off it went. I ignored her attempt to end our meeting.

"Look, Ms. Steinway, I need a job! I have three kids at home, and I need real benefits. I'm parked in a garage with no money to get out, my car is out of gas, and my unemployment checks are about to run out. I busted my butt to get here, and it sure wasn't for you to tell me it was all a mistake." I regretted every word that left my lips. Any minute, I anticipated her calling *security* and throwing me out of her office.

To my surprise, she didn't.

She clasped her hands together matter-of-factly. "I see. I'm sorry about your circumstances. I wish there was something I could do for you, but my hands are tied. The job is filled." She moved, as if to see me out.

I remained seated and swiveled the chair around. "There has to be another opening. Please. I'm a fast learner. I can pick up on things really easy." I hated the desperation in my voice and the fact I couldn't stop the tears from pooling in my eyes.

She hesitated, then sat back down at her cherry oak desk, put her glasses on and opened up a folder.

I sat there waiting, while my knee bounced up and down like a jackhammer.

After a few minutes, she said, "Let's see, you have a college education and solid office experience. Other than management openings, we have a mail clerk position, which you are overqualified for. It doesn't pay what this job was offering. Are you still interested?"

I sat there wondering what the hell was wrong with me considering a mail clerk position. If I wanted to deliver mail, I would have applied at the post office! And then, without warning, my body temperature rose about twenty degrees. A small fire burned within. I tried to keep it at bay, but this time, it was in full effect and it was going to run its course. I wanted to disrobe, as each piece of clothing acted like insulation. Water droplets blanketed my face and my eyes were clouded with sweat and tears. I took out some tissues. Ms. Steinway leaned back in her chair until the whole embarrassing episode had passed.

From somewhere under her desk – probably a private fridge – she produced a bottle of water. She placed it in front me with a sympathetic look, perhaps a peace offering.

My lips longed for a drink, but my pride and ego were black and blue, bruised from the news of someone else stealing *my* job.

She came around from the back of her desk and leaned against it facing me. She held her reading glasses in her hand.

"The change of life can be both liberating and depressing. The female body, once alive with life giving forces now ceases to be able to produce a human being. What is left is the residue of what once was. The fire and heat burn through you now, often feeling like hell itself has claimed you as its own. But that is not true. This process is actually alleviating you from responsibility and obligation. If you are not already, soon you will be free – free to wear that white dress, bathing suit or cream-colored outfit without fear of them being ruined. No more checking in the mirror, looking at your seat when you get up, or trying to conceal those extra little things in your purse."

She returned to her desk and sat down. "I know this little speech has nothing to do with you getting a job. You are a bit young to be going through a change of life, but life has a way of planning things for you."

She exhaled. "The fact of the matter is I've been forced to hire my wayward niece for the position. Without going further into the details, and I've said way too much already, I have to do what I have to do."

CHAPTER 7

I tried to digest everything she said while she dug in her file drawer, opening random files, finally settling on one that she placed on the desk in front of me.

"I do feel quite badly about this. It is probably hard to believe, but I wasn't always successful. I built this business with my partners from the ground up. I really can sympathize with your plight.

"You know, yours was not the only resume I received for this position. When Mr. Porter told me you were here, I was caught off guard. I quickly thumbed through all of the resumes and yours was stuck to someone else's. All of the other ones had the date and time of the rejection phone call, except for yours. Maybe it is fate."

I said a silent prayer that somehow I was going to come out of this victorious, even though I already felt defeated.

"I'm a pretty good judge of character, and I can't explain it, but I have a good feeling about you, Jerilyn. I like your forthright tenacity! I do have a job opening for a Personal Assistant.

"It has nothing to do with this company. I've been toying with the idea of having another 'right hand' as mine seems to not be able to keep up with all of my activities, but this would be temporary at first. I can pay you as an independent contractor, however, I would require that you work for me for six months and not look for another job during that time."

She opened the file folder for me, which contained some typed notes.

"These are some of the possible duties, which is really sort of a wish-list of what I would require. Look it over and let me know what you think." She turned to her computer and began typing.

I glanced at the paper. A lot of it was personal indeed – cleaners, hair and massage appointments, personal bills and invoice reconciliation, grocery shopping, travel arrangements, along with a few other tasks. What was I going to be? The help?

I found my voice, "Why can't your niece be *this* assistant?"

"That's simple: she's not qualified."

I challenged her. "But she is qualified to work here at this company? Really, I don't get it."

She kept typing without looking my way, "Quite frankly, it is not for you to *get*. I'm throwing you a life raft and it seems you're poking holes in it."

I noticed she got defensive but I wasn't going to back down. I surely didn't have anything to lose. "I'm just trying to understand the situation. I mean where will I work from? Would I meet you here every day?"

"I have a home office you can use." She paused briefly. "You know where Courtland Gardens is?"

Well, I shouldn't have been surprised that she lived in such an upscale neighborhood, right in the same vicinity as Palisades. The problem was me getting there without a car. I took the water bottle and swallowed several gulps. It was indeed icy cold and it felt good, even though the internal fire had passed.

I made up my mind and stood up. "Thanks, but no thanks."

CHAPTER 8

She stopped typing. "Jerilyn, what is the problem? I do pay quite well."

"I, I don't have a way to get there," I stammered. "I'm using my sister's car right now. No city bus goes to *The Gardens*."

"I see." She tapped her finger on her keyboard. "I'd be willing to send my car for you."

"Really?" I smirked. "Do you know where I live? Are you sure your driver can handle *my neighborhood*?"

My *hood* was Franklin Heights, about a mile from Petworth, home of a few blue collar retirees, low-income workers, lots of Section 8 housing and a liquor store every other corner. Drug dealers were prevalent but for the most part, if you minded your own business and acted like you belonged, you'd be okay. The demographics were about seventy percent Black and thirty percent Latino. I was stuck there because of my financial situation. There were worse places but Franklin Heights certainly wasn't anybody's tourist destination.

She became quite terse. "Ms. Jerilyn, if you have another prospect or job lead, I suggest you follow up on it.

I've gone above and beyond the call of duty and quite frankly, your sarcasm is not appreciated. I've tried to make this right. Believe it or not, I know *exactly* where you live. I said I'd send my driver for you…I didn't say to your house! He would pick you up from here. The city bus comes here, doesn't it? You know, the pride of your heart has deceived you!"

Boy, she blessed me out without uttering one curse word! And then had nerve to pull out what sounded like a Bible verse. It shocked me and at the same time, it reminded me of my faith. I regrouped my emotions and sat back down.

"I'm sorry. It's just that it has been a heck of a day. Can I have some time to think about it?"

She peered at me. "Excuse me, but what do you have now – perhaps an unemployment check? Seems if someone was smart, they could still get that check, since I'm paying you off the books." She turned back to her computer. "I need an answer right now. Otherwise, the offer is off the table."

I thought about what she was saying. Since she was paying me under the table, maybe I could even get ahead if I got approved for another extension on my unemployment checks.

I took another sip of water. "So for tax purposes, you wouldn't issue me a 1099?"

She smiled. "You are smart, aren't you? I wouldn't do that unless it became a permanent assignment. We can cross that bridge *if* and when we get to it."

I swallowed hard. Part of me wanted to decline, but once again, I was stuck in quicksand without a rope. I closed my eyes, praying for guidance, but deep down, I already knew the answer and had to retract what I said earlier. "Okay, when would I start?"

She nodded. "Ah, you finally see the light."

CHAPTER 9

I departed her office with a Monday start date. I wanted to bolt out of there, but I left with my head held high. Even though it was gainful employment, I kept feeling like I was pickin' cotton, modern day style.

I closed her office door behind me and stood near Porter's vacant desk collecting myself. Porter came back with some papers in his hand. I was happy to see he was about my sister's height, but I was also uptight. I cut my eyes at him.

"You knew, didn't you?"

He shook his head, looking perplexed. "Knew what? How did your interview go?"

"Cut the bull. She hired someone else."

"Oh wow. I'm sorry."

I leaned into him. "Didn't you make all of the rejection phone calls? Don't you set up all of her appointments? "

"No, not all of them. Human Resources normally handle the ones related to job interviews. Hmmm… yours was still on my calendar. I'm sorry you didn't get the job." He looked sincere, and I reeled in my claws.

"I got a job all right, but I won't be working here. She hired her niece for this position next to you." I waved in the direction of the empty desk.

He shrugged his shoulders. "You know blood's thicker than water. She probably hasn't had a chance to let me know."

I tried a little flirtation. "I was hoping to get to you know you better too, you know, hear more about your story, surviving the hurricane and all."

He smiled. "You can check me out anytime." Porter slid me a promo card for a local jazz club. "I sing with a band on the weekends called the Blu Bayou. That promo card entitles you to a two-for-one entry into the club. It's a twenty-five and over, old-school throw-back party. C'mon down and bring a friend, and don't forget your I.D."

"Okay, cool. I might check you out this weekend – if I can get a sitter." I was hittin' on him but he wasn't reciprocating. *Was it the sitter comment?* My gay-dar meter wasn't going off either.

There were a few moments of awkward silence; then his phone rang and he excused himself, answering it promptly. That was my cue to leave.

I walked back to the parking garage depressed. Porter didn't even act interested. I got in the car and looked at myself in the visor mirror. I looked terrible. My eyes were puffy and my eyeliner had smudged under both eyes. I started to bawl. I cried so hard my head hurt. I was going to be this woman's gopher, her glorified maid. But I needed the money, dammit, I needed the money. Speaking of which, she'd fronted me ten dollars to get out of this godforsaken garage. I hated taking it, but I was up against a rock and a hard place, my usual corner.

After a good ten minutes of feeling sorry for myself, I got it together. I needed to count my blessings. I had a lot of things to get in order, like daycare for the kids. I did pray for a job and I got one…it just wasn't the one I wanted.

I turned the key. It coughed and sputtered. I tried it again. Nothing. The tank was bone dry.

ANTOINE

CHAPTER 10

I had to have her!

I finished up my cigarette as I observed her from a distance.

Damn, she was fine! I got a hard-on just watchin' her.

I put my hand on my crotch tryin' to control my premature excitement. I could picture myself inside of her, learnin' every inch of her sexy body. Out of all of my victories, this would be the one to put me on the map!

The *she* was a Mercedes SL 550 Roadster. It was painted a custom, deep burgundy. It belonged to Chaz Rosen, an employee of one of the many businesses next to the garage.

Chaz didn't need it and his insurance would replace it. On the other hand, I needed it badly.

Jo-Jo was my boy who specialized in stolen identities. His business was a serious moneymakin' operation. Before I jacked a car, I always had him run the plates 'cause you never know how many of us could get paid from one rich prick. Right there on the screen, he pulled up Chaz's license, with his social security number and address. Havin' all that personal info was like putty in Jo- Jo's hands. Jo-Jo accessed Chaz' bank accounts, credit cards, real estate holdin's, and court records. Chaz had over a hundred thousand dollars in the bank, cash! His credit was perfect, hell, his life was perfect. Well I was about to rip apart his fairy tale. Not only was Chaz's car about to go bye-bye, his little nest egg would soon follow.

Stealin' this beauty was gonna be a challenge. I had studied it inside and out. Chaz had two alarms on his ride – one custom device that notified him if anyone so much as touched it. I knew this because I purposely set off the alarm. I had taken my hand and stroked it, startin' with the hood, workin' my way down the side to the back of the trunk. I noticed a light on the dashboard turned from red to green. But the car was silent.

I stood back and watched the action. I needed to know how long it took him to get to the car, what he did to turn it off, and what he did to reset it.

It took him fifteen minutes to get to the vehicle. Chaz arrived lookin' mad as shit. He wasn't that tall, maybe five-foot-six, a buck fifty soakin' wet. His glasses made him look like he was an accountant, but he was a third generation lawyer.

First, he carefully examined the car, walkin' around it, starin' at it like it was about to come to life. After he was satisfied, he used his remote entry and when the car door opened, it made a high pitched sound that he turned off and reset. His cell phone rang – somebody lookin' for him. He told them he had to check out his car – *his baby*. Satisfied, he left the scene.

The next week, I bumped the shit out of it, careful not to leave a dent. It went off like a police siren. This time, Chaz was there in eight minutes flat. Clearly, the first time he was in a meetin' or somethin'; maybe there was some sort of delay with that silent alarm. But that bump brought his ass runnin' like the damn cavalry. Again, he examined the car inch by inch. He cussed aloud, mumblin' about all the money he paid for *this faulty alarm system*. Said he was gonna get a camera. Finally, he left.

So now I knew that I had a minimum of eight minutes to crack the code and as much as maybe 15 minutes, but I would shave that down to ten minutes max! I was goin' to have to be damn near perfect but the reward was goin' to be great. And I had to do it before he installed his next antitheft device.

And if Chaz rolled up on me, or if anyone else did, there'd be hell to pay.

Brand new, the car was in the low six figures. Chico's chop shop had already promised me sixty large if it was in top notch condition. Gettin' out of the garage should be a piece of cake because Chaz had a monthly pass that electronically let him in and out. All I had to do was start the car, drive normal and not get caught!

I started my stopwatch and went to work. With my glass cutter, I made a perfect circle in the driver's window that I could reach through. Surely the proximity alarm would let Chaz know that his car was bein' fucked with. The ODB port was easily accessible, and that's where I plugged in my favorite toy.

The blank key fob I had with me was programmed for his keyless entry and ignition and in just a few seconds, I unlocked the car as if I owned it. This was only part one. If I didn't disable the alarm, he'd still have a string attached. I popped the hood, and pulled the fuses for the alarm system. Bingo! I still had three minutes to spare. I hopped in.

I paced myself drivin' down from the sixth floor of the garage, although I wanted to hurry up and fly down those windin' curves and hit the exit and get paid! So far, everything was goin' perfectly. I turned the radio on, changed the station from that classical crap to somethin' more urban, and Meek Mill's *I'ma Boss* was playin'...*ain't that the truth*?

When I got to the exit level, there was a three-car-deep backup. The damn scanner wasn't workin' and the dude, Mitchell, had to manually raise the arm and let you out. His old, white ass seemed to be talkin' to every last person like he was their best friend.

I had very little options at this point. I could throw the car in park and run like hell or I could drive this bitch right through the gate. Of course, that would damage the hood.

Damaged goods always reduced the price big time! Replacin' the window was expected but not a damn hood!

I could not bring it in with a jacked up hood. There was already a wager on me not makin' this happen but they should-a known better. I was now only two cars away from freedom. I put on my shades and oversized baseball cap. My stopwatch was down to thirty seconds.

My heart was thumpin' at a steady, accelerated pace,

but I wasn't the least bit afraid – just the opposite. It was all a rush and that is what kept me locked in the game.

I had the tinted windows rolled halfway down to partially hide the hole, while I got closer to Mitchell. I held my heat in my lap.

"Hey, Mr. Ro..." He was shocked to see me. "You're not Mr. Rosen."

"You're right. I'm not." I tried to keep my head down low. "He asked me to get his car detailed for him."

He was not convinced. "Really? Look, Mr. Rosen don't let nobody drive his car! Why don't we call him, shall we?" He started thumbin' through some papers lookin' for Chaz' phone number.

I closed my eyes. Shit!

"Mitchell! Fuckin' look at me!"

Mitchell eyes widened when he saw the thirty-eight pointed at him while the cars in back of me became impatient and started a horn symphony.

"Open this damn gate and you'll see another day. Do anythin' different, and I'ma blast ya ass into next week. Now open the fuckin' gate!"

He had his hands raised, tryin' to bring attention to the situation and started stallin', "Don't hurt me. Don't shoot."

In my rear view mirror, I saw a glimpse of a man runnin' toward us, yellin'. It had to be that damn Chaz!

I cocked the gun. "You got five seconds, Mitchell. Four, three, two..."

The arm went up and I floored the pedal.

CHAPTER 11

I exited the garage like an escaped slave, movin' fast and with purpose. D.C. streets were tough to speed in, but I had already mapped out three different ways to get to home base. Soon, I got comfortable and was able to cruise the rest of the way.

Twenty minutes later when I pulled into the garage, the five-man crew stood there in shock. When I got out, they all applauded.

Now *that's* what I'm talkin' 'bout. They quickly locked down all the doors then dismantled any tracking devices.

Chico, covered in grime, grease and paint, rolled over to me and gave me a fist pound.

"Holy shit! You really did the damn thin'. Look at this here! Hot damn!" Chico, a Black Puerto Rican, walked around the vehicle, noddin' his approval.

He looked at me like a proud father. "I am fuckin' impressed! Ant, I can't believe it. This shit is da bomb!"

"Hell yeah, I did it. And y'all mo-fo's owe me some money!" They all laughed givin' me props, fillin' my pockets with their twenty dollar bets, except for Shaina.

Me and Chico went way back. We met in prison. We were both in there 'cause we did some dumb shit. We became fast friends and never lost contact.

Shaina, the butch in the crew, rolled her eyes. I didn't give a damn that her body work experience was like no other I ever seen. We had nothin' but bad blood 'tween us. She was five-ten and tatted up. If she ever was pretty, that shit was erased by her blond buzz cut and masculine muscles.

She stood there in green overalls and a backwards blue N.Y. Yankees baseball cap. "Who gonna buy this shit Chico? It's too hot. Ain't nobody gonna give you what you want for it."

I lit up a cigarette and blew smoke in her face. "Leave it to you to ruin the mood. Ain't nobody asked you anyway! My ass is here to collect! Tell her, Chico."

Chico grinned. "I got you, homey, you know that. Don't listen to Shaina. You know she's a jealous hoe."

Shaina stared at me. "How much you think you gonna get, Ant?"

"At least sixty."

"You a bigger fool than you look."

"Fuck you, Shaina! Why don't you go and fix the damn window? Ain't that what you get paid to do? C'mon Chico, let's square up."

She just shook her head as me and Chico walked to his office and closed the door.

CHAPTER 12

Chico's government name was Charles Benitez. His papa, Paulie, was a rollin' stone and his mama was one of Paulie's chicks on the side. He liked them young, sexy and fine, but they had to be legal. Chico's mom was a dark-skinned beauty who was fast, wild and loose. She hung out at the garage a lot and Paulie started buyin' her gifts and givin' her money. Next thing you know, she and Paulie were lovers and Chico came along. Paulie stayed involved in their lives and taught Chico and his half-brother, Raoul, everything about cars. Papa's dream was to open his own mechanic's business; he wanted somethin' he could pass down to his two favorite sons, and after he had scrimped and saved, he bought a place and named it Benitez & Sons, which was a legitimate operation.

Paulie thought he was doin' everything right to keep his sons out of the thug life and that's what they led him to believe, until Raoul got gunned down in a hail of bullets due to gang violence. It broke Paulie's heart to lose a son to the streets, and he made Chico promise not to follow in Raoul's footsteps.

Chico kept his promise – until his father died of lung cancer from his pack-a-day habit. There was no real money in fixin' people's cars. Sure, he did it to maintain a realistic cover but car jackin' paid the bills.

We were now in his office where he conducted all of his deals. It made him feel like a legitimate businessman, even tho he was far from it. The office was dark and dated with wood paneling, and a few framed photos of his family hung on the wall – but mostly pictures of him and his dad. The furnishings were from his father's time in the shop – the same rickety desk that rocked back and forth because the floor was unleveled. Stacks of files, in no particular order, sat at the corner of the desk; a tall file cabinet was up against the wall, along with a mini fridge that had a small television on top. He had an old Nintendo game system hooked up to that.

Chico rolled a joint. "Ant, I gotta admit, we ain't think you was gonna pull this off." He lit it up and took a puff. I took one too.

"Well I did it. You got a buyer lined up?"

"About that." Another puff exchanged between us. "I do have a buyer lined up and he's still interested, but he only wants to cough up forty."

"What?" I just knew I did not hear him correctly.

"Look, like I said, we had no idea you was gonna make this happen and in good condition. So I hadda allow for damages. Can you understand that?"

The fire rose up in me like an explodin' volcano. Shaina knew what she was talkin' about and that shit burned me up.

The problem was that she *always* knew what she was talkin' about.

I leaned forward. "We should hold out then. Somebody gonna pay top dollar for that. We can't take nothin' less than sixty or seventy. C'mon, don't do this to me."

Chico inhaled and shook his head. "Look, we gotta get rid of this ride, man. We should take the forty and you know it." He passed the weed to me but I waved it off.

"And what will I get?" I was on the edge of my seat about to come across the desk. "I did all the damn work, as usual. This is some bullshit!"

"Calm down, Antoine." He leaned back in his secondhand leather office chair with the missin' armrest. "I'm not gonna take my usual cut. You'll walk away with about twenty-five. And you know outta my piece, I gotta pay the crew, so I'm the one on the losin' end."

I could not hold in my anger. "Fuck you, how's that?"

His eyes were now little red slits. "Where else you gonna walk away with twenty-five large? This is a good deal. Take it."

I exhaled, feelin' mellow from the weed, but you shouldn't mess with a man's money. Chico should know that shit! And that car was worth way more than some lousy forty g's!

He got up and went to his fridge and pulled out two Caronas, but I wasn't in a drinkin' mood. He popped the cap and threw it on the floor. "Look, next time, we'll believe it when you say you gonna go fast and furious on me." He took a long swig.

"What if I don't wanna deal? What if I find my own buyer?"

He rolled his eyes. "You know it don't work that way, Ant. I know you upset, I can see that. I fucked up. I made a promise I can't keep. You really shocked the shit outta me. Look, it won't happen again."

"You damn skippy it ain't! I'm takin' the car."

CHAPTER 13

That made Chico's blood boil. "You ain't takin' a got-damn thing! I don't know where you get off thinkin' you runnin' things! This is the first nice ride you brought here since you started jackin' cars. Get the hell outta my face. You ain't takin' shit!"

Chico's whole disposition changed. For seven years, we'd been boys, but right now, we were about to go at it.

I stood up. "Watch me."

"Antoine, you don't wanna do this. What the hell's gotten into you? C'mon. We boys! Agree to twenty-five and bounce!"

I slammed my hands on the desk. "We boys? Is that what you said? Who da hell out there is risking they damn life on these vehicles? Y'all sit here behind the scenes, sittin' on ya ass all protected 'n shit. My ass is on the line! You promised me a big payday, Chico. This shit ain't right." I rubbed my forehead, which was throbbin' like a marching band.

"Who the hell wouldn't take this kinda cash? Do you hear yo self? In a few days, ya money will be here. Cold hard cash! Is ya ass on crack or somethin'? You got a drug problem? How the fuck's this ain't enough money?"

I was hot! I had big plans with that money. First, I was movin' into a rent-to-own condo. I had already put down five thousand dollars, but because my credit was fucked up, I needed another ten to close the deal and I only had thirty days to get it. So how was I gonna take care of business with twenty-five grand? I had a high maintenance girlfriend and my dumb-ass promised her a five thousand dollar shopping spree. I had shit on layaway – big screens, sound systems, appliances. I had to take care of my son. I wanted custody of him because his psycho mother had him on some fucked-up medication. I needed him to have his own room. Now this dude had me looking like a fool!

Chico was jokin' about me being on crack, but some of it rang true. I wasn't the one with the habit; it was my girl. She liked that weed and was messin' with oxy, and who knew what else. Been tryin' to slow her ass down with no success.

It was hard jackin' cars! Technology was messin' up everything. I pulled this particular job 'cause I was guaranteed a nice payday, which would have kept me away from that life long enough for me to figure out my next big move.

I tried to reason with him. "Lemme have five days to find my own buyer, and we'll all make out better than this fucked-up deal you made."

He took exception to my insult. "What is it you ain't understandin'? I already promised the car to someone else, and he's gonna be here in three days, after the new paint job cures out and shit. I ain't gonna say this again, Ant. You really startin' to get on my fuckin' nerves!" He finished off his beer and popped open the other bottle.

"What about the promise you made me?" I was slowly feelin' beaten. "That don't mean shit, do it?"

"Ant, look, I'm sorry, okay? You ain't takin' the car and if you keep talkin' shit, I'ma take my normal cut. Now get the fuck outta my office."

I shook my head. "This is fucked up! I'll be back in three days for my money."

"Finally! My nigga. Now *that's* what I'm talkin' 'bout!" He had his fist out for a pound and I ignored it.

"What time's the buyer comin'?'"

"Uh, he should be here 'round six. That's what he said. Stop by 'round seven and we'll square up."

I stood up. "I'm done wit'cha ass, Chico."

He shrugged his shoulders. "You just mad. When you down to yo last dollar, you'll be back."

JERILYN

CHAPTER 14

After I left Ms. Steinway, I had to call my sister and let her know I ran out of gas. I was still an emotional wreck and she could hear the sadness in my voice while I kept apologizing. She was amazingly calm – probably because she had roadside assistance. Thirty minutes later, I was gassed up and headed back home, working out childcare in my head as I drove.

It was easy getting childcare for my girls. The woman upstairs, Miss Cora, had a 24-hour daycare and she was trustworthy and reasonable. She'd would watch them for a week until they could attend a church-run camp that offered a partial financial scholarship. Placing DeMarcus was a different matter altogether but doable. Because he was a special needs child, the District helped out a lot. So I was able to enroll him in a summer program for mentally challenged children free of charge. I'd done this before and once DeMarcus was on his meds on a regular basis, he'd notice that he was among "problem" children and wanted out. In this case, I poured my heart out to the camp administrator, telling her the problems with my ex. The camp had different levels of care and they assured me if DeMarcus became "well", they'd would make him a helper and give him other incentives to not feel out of place. Only time would tell.

It was Saturday night, and I was going out to celebrate before my first day of slave labor working for "Ms. Daisy." I had on my club gear – black spandex, gold, four-inch wedge sandals, and a white halter top that concealed my tummy pouch adequately. I piled my locs high on top of my head, in what I considered a fashionable bun and added some gold hoop earrings.

Carmella and I were going to the jazz club to check out Porter and his band with the few dollars I had left from my check. A few minutes earlier, I dropped the kids with Miss Cora for four hours. I couldn't afford more than that for three children; after midnight, I would incur a crazy late fee.

Everybody loved Miss Cora. She was our resident "nanny" with a short, round body and bright eyes that sparkled through her oversized bifocals. She kept her hair in a messy ponytail that hung down her back from her half Native American dad and creole mother. She was a beauty back in her day.

She owned her own daycare center for years, which took advantage of her teaching credentials. But when her mother took ill, she moved her daycare into her detached home so she could care for her until her death.

No one remembered much about her husband. It was said that one day she came home from the store and he was gone and never came back.

Eventually, managing the house became too much and she moved into the spacious three-bedroom apartment above mine, but she always cared for kids, employing her niece, Letesha, as her trustworthy assistant. When she moved in years ago, this was a nice area.

She had helped raise many of the kids in the neighborhood, including her own boys who graduated at the top of their class in law school and ran their own practice in New York. Her boys wanted her to move out of the neighborhood and to come east with them but she refused, saying "we" needed her.

Miss Cora was cool with DeMarcus but only in short stints. In this case, I had all three arrive in their pajamas. The next day, after my interview and Carmella playing nanny, she introduced me to Melatonin, a natural sleep aid for DeMarcus. I was against it, but tonight, I used it to stay in Cora's good graces and to keep him calm.

As usual, Carmella was late and she knew I was on a tight leash. I rang her cell phone and it went to voicemail. I texted her: *hurry your ass up*.

Almost twenty minutes after that, she texted me to come downstairs. I was livid. I locked up and took the decrepit elevator and hopped in the messy car, after I threw the two empty bags of Doritos to the back seat.

I slammed the door. "What the hell took you so long?"

"Put your seatbelt on and calm down! I broke a nail and had to get it fixed! I mean considering the time, I did damn good."

I shook my head. "I have to be back by midnight or else I gotta pay a hellacious late fee."

She giggled. "Okay, Cinderella, I'll have you home in time before you turn into a pumpkin."

I did not laugh at her weak joke. "Please, just get us there."

CHAPTER 15

Parking near the club was tricky, but we lucked up on someone leaving and we eased into their spot just a block from the club.

There was a line to get in. We had to get past the two-man security team, who looked like a couple of black Sumo wrestlers, about six-five each. The promo card being a two-for-one, we were shocked when they asked for forty dollars. While Carmella worked at the hospital, she liked really nice things, like gold jewelry and designer handbags. She had her own apartment and a car payment. Basically, she was always borderline broke!

My sister mouthed off, "Better be worth it or else I want my money back!" We pieced together the money, realizing we were down to getting one drink between us, if that.

One of the Sumo twins brusquely responded, "No refunds."

I ushered Carmella into the club before her mouth got us turned away.

I finally paid attention to what my sister was wearing – a sleeveless leopard print mini spandex dress that had a moderate V-neck in the front and a sheer back; her breasts stood at attention. She had on low wedge black sandals that wrapped around the ankle and large black dangling earrings. Her hair was straight and her face was fresh, with just a touch of mascara and lip gloss. I was quite jealous.

I followed her to a corner table where we could barely see the band, but I immediately spotted Porter on the split level keyboards. The dance floor was packed; the band transitioned to *Before I Let Go* by Maze featuring Frankie Beverly.

Our parents always had music in the house, preferring old-school soul; we knew all of the hot jams from the seventies on up and even some from the sixties.

My sister jumped up. "That's my jam." And before I knew it, she was on the dance floor groovin' by herself – but not for long. Some dude immediately joined her and that was typical for Carmella.

I grooved in my seat; of course, no one asked me to dance. A waitress came by asking if I wanted a drink. Upon hearing a white wine spritzer was twelve dollars, I declined.

I suddenly regretted being there. I should've saved my money. But I hardly went out as it was. Who was I kidding? Porter couldn't care less if I was here or not. Even though the band was jammin', I started to feel a bit blue.

I checked my phone for random text messages and Facebook updates. Nothing new to report, except that we had to roll outta there in less than an hour. I looked up and saw Carmella and her newfound friend coming toward the table as the band took a fifteen minute break and put on a mixed tape.

Carmella was glistening. "Jerilyn, meet T-Bone. T-Bone, this is my sister, Jerilyn," she said grinnin' like she was in a Crest commercial.

I raised an eyebrow. "T-Bone? Like the steak?"

He laughed. "Yeah, my grandmomma said I was born with the shape of one on my backside and the name stuck all these years." He wiped the sweat off his bald head with a hankie. "Name's William." He held out his hand and I shook his fingertips.

"I see." I found the conversation a bit weird but Carmella wasted no time.

"It's hotter than a jalapeno up in here! I could sure use a drink." She fanned herself.

T-Bone smiled a toothy grin. "My pleasure. What shall it be?"

Carmella quickly responded, "I'll just take a Coke, but have the waiter bring it to the table." We'd learned early on not to trust nobody with your drink.

Eager to please, he said, "Be right back." The well-dressed middle-aged man went off to the bar. He was a little taller than Carmella, and stocky but looked fit, with good definition and smooth skin. I thought it was rude that he didn't also offer me a drink but then my whole mood was in the dumps.

She turned her attention to me. "Girl, you don't look so good." She plopped down in the seat next to mine.

"Well, I gotta leave soon. And this ain't all it's cracked up to be."

"Damn! You need to get it together. This party is just gettin' started. You haven't even talked to that Porter dude yet. Shoot, you may hafta go home in a cab. All that money we paid to get in here? Girl, puh-leez."

The mixed tape started a round of popular line dances. "C'mon Jerilyn." She dragged me onto the dance floor and T-Bone soon joined us, coming between me and Carmella. I finished out the *Electric Slide* and headed to the restroom.

On my way back, I saw a familiar face at the bar. It was definitely Elise, and she was hanging all over some man she had no business being with. I used my cellphone camera and snapped several incriminating shots. She looked drunk as hell and the dude was all over her like they had history with each other. What a skank!

The band was heading back to the stage and Porter walked right by me. I called out to him, "Hey Porter."

He turned around and looked at me as if I was a stranger. Then he recognized me. "Jerilyn, right? You're lookin' good. Glad you could make it."

He was again sharply dressed, in pressed denim jeans, white shirt, skinny red tie and a black leather vest. He smelled so good.

I smiled, "Yeah, I'm here with my sister, but I can't stay much longer."

"Well, we play here every second Saturday of the month and we're trying to add another date. Usually we reach capacity by eleven. This is a light crowd tonight."

I kept grinning, trying to look cute. "I don't know where you could fit another person. It's already packed. I'm glad I get to see you do your thing."

"I'm getting ready to do my *thang* again! Check me out. Hey, did you and your sister want to come to the after party?"

"Where would that be at?" I asked as if I didn't have three children waitin' at home.

"There's an upper level here, but it is by invitation only. If y'all here at 2 AM, c'mon upstairs. I'll let you in."

I wanted to introduce him to my sister, but he was gone. I tried to be happy, but I couldn't pull it off, as he headed back to the stage.

I glanced at my watch. We needed to leave like right now.

CHAPTER 16

I made my way back to the dance floor, where I'd left Carmella, but she was nowhere to be found.

Porter had the mic. He broke out in an old Keith Sweat song and was doing it justice. Ladies were callin' out his name, so clearly he was well-known. No wonder I'm the farthest thing from his mind. He could have any woman he wanted. I'd wasted enough time and where was that damn Carmella?

"Can I get this dance, young lady?" I looked up to find a Black Colonel Sanders trying to get his groove on.

"Uh, no thanks. Another time." He looked disappointed and moved on. Figures I'd attract somebody's grandfather.

Finally, I saw Carmella, still with T-Bone. I ran up and interrupted her, lookin' like a dance contestant. "Girl, we gotta roll."

"Look, I'm not leaving. No way. Let's get you a cab." She spun around me like a spinning top. I moved closer to her, mad as shit!

"You do this crap every time! We agree to a plan and you flake on it. I barely had enough money to get in here. You know I don't have money for a cab! Damn, Carmella!"

She stopped dancing and spoke to T-Bone, "Can you believe this?"

Why is she dragging this stranger in our business?

T-Bone said, "I'll take you home."

My sister and I both looked at T-Bone like he grew a third eye. Carmella shook her head. "Hold up! We don't know you like that!"

He put his hands up., "Hey, calm down. I'm just trying to help."

I yelled at Carmella, "We came together and we leavin' together!" I grabbed her elbow and she snatched away.

"You ain't my mama! I don't have chick nor child." She started diggin' in her purse. "I'm-a find you some cab money!"

I had smoke coming out of my nostrils. "It's at least thirty dollars. You don't have it!"

T-Bone extended his hand. "Here's forty dollars. You can pay me back. And here's my business card. I'm a financial analyst for Bay City Financial. I've been there ten years. Really, take the money. Y'all wastin' time arguing over nothin' but a few dollars. Just call me when you have the money."

Carmella folded her arms. "There! Problem solved! Now go home to your children."

I was so mad, I was hyperventilating. "You just said we don't know him like that! You are pickin' him over me? How low can you go? I don't want his charity! All he wants is some ass!"

T-Bone shook his head. "What's your name again? Geraldine? I don't appreciate that jacked-up comment. You need to check yourself!"

Carmella snatched the money out of his hand and shoved it in mine, dragging me to the front door. "Take the fuckin' money. And by the way, Porter is gay! Stevie Wonder could have seen that! Now what I do with my ass is my business, and you know I don't roll like that. Either way, I ain't leavin'. You got ten minutes before you turn into a pumpkin. You gonna stay or you gonna roll?"

CHAPTER 17

Angry did not adequately explain how I felt riding in the back of Jimmy's Black-Ice Sedan Service. It was 12:05 AM, and I was five dollars into late fees and counting at one dollar a minute.

I called Miss Cora.

"Hey Jerilyn baby. You almost here?"

"Not really." I closed my eyes, trying not to bust out crying. "I'll be there in about fifteen minutes. I know I owe you that late fee, and I'm sorry."

"Don't worry about it this time. These kids was no problem at all. DeMarcus been sleep almost since he got here. I'll let you slide this time. I know you don't get out much."

Her kindness touched me and calmed me down a bit. "Thank you so much, Miss Cora. You don't know how much I appreciate that."

"I'll get them ready. Letesha will be here to greet you. Take care."

We hung up the phone and it started again, that unnerving prickly sensation all over my upper body. I tried to stop it from happening, but it was already on its way. The air-conditioning was on but it was no match for what my body was about to unleash. The warmth crawled up between my shoulder blades as if someone had just dropped hot lava on the back of my neck. My breast area radiated steam, and I blinked away the sweat and tears as they kissed each other sliding down my face. I took out a tissue from my purse and intended to dab my skin but it just slid across my forehead as if on an oil slick. I cussed under my breath; I damned my ancestors for this early menopause curse that affected my mother and her mother before her. I blamed Mother Nature, Adam and Eve for the suffering that all women endured. And in the same breath, I prayed for deliverance from the internal fire that burned within me, like a tray of smoldering charcoal.

ANTOINE

CHAPTER 18

It was three days later. Me and my boy, Kinnard, had been sittin' outside Chico's since 3 PM in my girl's 1990 black Grand Prix that was on its last leg. Even though it was mid-June and summer had not fully arrived, the inside-a that car was like bein' in a sauna. The A/C worked sporadically and today was definitely an *off* day. Kinnard's deodorant gave out long ago. We talked about our history together, constantly reminiscin' on the same stupid things. I was tired of sittin' in the car with him and volunteered to do any snack trips to the nearby store just to get some fresh air. We started out with water, which turned to Gatorade and then inevitably Heineken.

I had really good gut instincts that I never used to listen to. But for the most part, that stint in prison taught me a valuable lesson.

I'd told Kinnard we should-a torched that car lot ourselves but he wanted to get that no good druggie, Malik, to do it – talkin' 'bout this way, our hands would be clean. My gut told me not to trust his plan but Kinnard seemed so damn sure!

When I was talkin' to Chico about the car deal, I got that strange feelin' in my gut again. Chico was lyin'. Ain't no way on this earth was that car goin' for forty grand. He was tryin' to dick me outta my money. And when I asked him what time was the deal goin' down, he hesitated. So I made sure I was on the scene way ahead of him and everybody knew Chico didn't step foot outta bed till noon.

Around 4:30 PM, everyone rolled outta the garage, like they were knockin' off early. I watched Chico do everything he normally does when he shuts down for the day, 'cept he left one-a the garage bays open.

Thirty minutes later, a white dude rolled up in a pearl Escalade. He was dressed sharply in a black three-piece suit. Me and Kinnard looked at each other and nodded in agreement that we thought he was the buyer.

Kinnard said, "Look at Three-piece. Where the hell did he think he was comin' to? His first date?" We laughed a bit.

Before I left outta the garage the other evenin', I used the restroom in the back. I jimmied the back door lock and that's how I was gonna slip in and observe the whole shit go down. It was supposed to be a fire exit. No one hardly used it, and I was bankin' on that. I moved quickly, but knew I had a few minutes 'cause no doubt, Three-piece was gonna examine that car with a fine-tooth comb.

We watched Three-piece knock on the entry door and eventually, Chico answered. They talked briefly then Three-piece got back in his ride and drove into the empty garage bay.

As the garage bay closed down, I made my move. I eased my way inside and into Chico's office. He'd left the radio playin' some Latino club music. I parked myself inside his free-standin' closet and waited. I really wanted to be wrong 'bout Chico but I knew different.

Standin' in that closet was hard work; I was sweatin' like a summertime marathon runner, and I was mixed in between his spare overalls that reeked of perspiration and cigarettes. There were two pairs of work boots that smelled like sour milk and made me wanna puke, but I was determined to find out the truth and swallowed my own spit to keep myself together.

Several minutes later, he and Three-piece walked into the office.

CHAPTER 19

The two men sat opposite each other, and I had a good view of them through the small crack in the door. Three-piece's hair was like black soot, shiny and slicked back.

He asked Chico, "Where's your crew?"

Chico lit up a cigarette. He reached over and turned up the radio, "Love this song! Reminds me of this girl, Jazmine, I used to date but gettin' back to you, look, they gone. I don't have 'em around when I'm doin' this type of bid'ness, know what I'm sayin'?" He blew a couple smoke rings.

Three-piece replied, "Smart man. I trust the car is clean?"

"Absolutely! All of our cars are scrubbed clean before they're delivered. Every fingerprint, dirt spec, and smudge mark has been eliminated. The VIN number is filed off; all trackin' devices destroyed. You can eat off it. Your boss knows my rep. And you know this car's worth six figures. All you gotta do now is get it home."

"That's not an issue. My boy, Drake, is waitin' for me to call him. You got that remote entry?"

"Only if you got that money."

"You mean that sixty-five thou in small bills you demanded?"

"Exactly."

I held my breath when I heard the amount. There is no honor among thieves!

"Well, Mr. Benitez, we got us a little problem."

Chico practically jumped out of his chair. "The hell we do! I delivered as promised. How's this shit a problem?"

"You seem to have short-term memory. You know we still got that outstanding debt for those drugs we fronted you. When you gonna settle up?"

"Things are slow, man." Chico's tune changed to Mr. Nice Guy. "I just need a little more time. Gimme a week then we can square up."

"A week?" Three-piece waved his finger back and forth. "The boss don't grant extensions."

"Whoa man, hold up. This deal right here is about the car. I still gotta pay the driver. Noboby said I needed to have that other stuff today. You know that's new territory for me. Matter fact, I got my boys out there right now tryin' to make that paper. I was also hopin' this car would earn me some favor. This shit wasn't easy."

Three-piece laughed. "You got your boys out there? Really? We know everybody on these streets. None of them look new. Are you lying to me right now?"

Chico got indignant and stood up. "My man, I think you need to leave. I'll finish this up with Mr. Russo."

Three-piece stood up, too, and shouted, "Sit'cha ass down!" The tone of his voice sent a shiver up my spine. I started to have a sinkin' feelin' about this whole shit.

Chico's eyes narrowed; he glared at Three-piece. They both sat back down together. Chico blew the last of his smoke toward Three-piece. "I don't like your attitude."

"I don't give a shit! You think you slick, don't you?"

"What the hell you talkin' 'bout?"

"Let me just cut to the chase. We're done doing business with you."

"Then how Russo gonna get paid?" Chico put out his cigarette.

"Well, you've become what we call a *liability*. Guess you didn't think we'd find out you've been working with our rival, the Alvarez Brothers. You know, money makes people talk and they talked a lot! Even have video footage – gotta love cell phones. So they are going to get *your* reward, which I'm going to deliver personally right after I leave here. But you, my friend, will never see a penny of it."

Three-piece pulled out his gun, equipped with a silencer.

Chico raised his hands. "Wait a minute."

Three-piece held his gun on Chico. "Give me the car keys."

He put his hands down and sounded desperate. "You listenin' to the Alvarez Brothers over me? I don't believe this shit! Get Mr. Russo on the phone!"

"I'm not gonna to ask you again."

Chico reached in his pocket mumblin' about how videos can be doctored and how he was framed. He started to slide the key across the desk, then called Three-piece's bluff. "You know what? Fuck you!"

"No, fuck *you*!"

The next few seconds took my breath away. Three-piece shot Chico dead with two bullets to the forehead.

CHAPTER 20

Me and Chico beefin' wasn't nothin' new and even tho he was low ballin' my cut, he ain't deserve to die like this. I had my gun on me but I never fired it. It was in case I had to. I wasn't a stone cold killer at heart; I was a thief.

The last time and probably the only time I was scared was in prison when my ass was tagged for a gang rape. That shit never happened but I was scared like a rabbit in a lion's den. I lost ten pounds in a week walkin' around freaked out that any minute now, I was goin' down. When Three-piece popped Chico, I was terrified. My whole body trembled and my gut twisted and cramped up like a bad case of stomach flu. But I had to keep it together or I'd be next.

I closed my eyes and controlled my breathin' as the assassin made a phone call.

"Hey, it's me. Yeah, he's done. He won't be stealing anything else from you. Yeah…he was in way over his head.

"I also picked up that package from Cheverly. Figure I'd kill two birds with one stone. I'm gonna go make good with Johnny Alvarez too.

"I plan on bringing the car tonight. I'm telling you, that car is nothing but the truth! I'll expect my usual fee. I'm out!"

It was only then that I noticed he had on leather gloves. Chico was probably dead no matter what he said. Three-piece ensured he left nothin' behind and exited the room.

When I felt sure he wasn't comin' back, I eased my way out of the closet. My clothes were stuck to me like fly paper. Clearly, Chico was into sum shit I ain't know about. This was bad all the way 'round.

I stared at his dead body as a burnin' tear rolled down my cheek. I wasn't one for cryin' but this shit just wasn't right. Now I was out of a job and I'd lost a friend. One thing was for sure. Three-piece was not gettin' outta that door without me gettin' somethin' for my troubles!

CHAPTER 21

I moved quietly from the back office to the main floor of the garage. He was already inside the vehicle. Damn! Then he got out of the car lookin' frustrated. He pushed the remote start a few times but the car would not catch.

I smiled to myself. Chico did somethin' to disable the vehicle. Probably did that all the time as a guarantee.

He opened the hood, lookin' for a clue, then said aloud, "Son of a bitch!"

He got back on the phone. "Drake, it's me… yeah, this Chico dude removed something, probably one of the sensors. I don't know where he could've put it. Don't worry, I'm going to figure this out. I'll call you when I get it going." He hung up.

He started to look around the shop, talkin' to himself. He was diggin' through every toolbox, throwin' shit all over the place. My phone was vibratin' in my pocket, and I moved farther toward the back. It was a text from Kinnard.

He wrote: *"Wat up? Les go."*

I texted him back: *"Not yet. Deal went bad."* Then I thought about it. *"Come nock on the door n act like u need help wit yr car. Do it now."*

"Wat?"

"Do it."

A short while later, Kinnard was bangin' on the door. Three-piece went to answer it with his gun drawn. Kinnard banged harder and started hollerin', "Hey Chico. I need some help wit my car. It's leakin' oil. C'mon man, lemme in, I know you in there."

Three-piece yelled back, "Yo, we closed. Come back tomorrow."

And that was when I bum-rushed him and clocked him on the back of his head with the butt of my gun. But unlike the movies, that fool was not out cold. He stumbled forward and fell to his knees, while his gun slid across the floor.

He looked at me and sputtered, "Who the fuck are you?"

Adrenaline took over. I kicked him in the head and stomped him in his gut. I quickly let Kinnard in.

Kinnard came inside, smellin' like overripe fruit. "Yo, I'm ready to get the…what the hell?" He looked back and forth between me and Three-piece, whose ass was crunched up on the floor, still moanin' and unable to get up.

I was outta breath. "This dude popped Chico. Chico's dead!"

Kinnard blinked. "No shit?" He shook his head, stunned. "Naw man, not Chico."

My body was a bundle of nerves. "I saw the whole thing hidin' in his office."

Three-piece tried to talk. Kinnard yelled at him, "Shut

the fuck up," and kicked him in his face, splittin' his lip and breakin' his nose. Then he was out cold.

My stomach was rumblin' like I'd eaten poisoned fish. "Kinnard, this shit's bad, really bad. This dude was hired to pop Chico and take the car. And he sounded like he was sayin' Chico was into sellin' drugs too."

"Well we got problems, don't we? Three-piece done seen our faces, Ant. We can't let him live."

CHAPTER 22

I heard what he said but I could not accept it. "Look, this ain't our thing. There's gotta be somethin' else we can do."

"Yeah, you right." Kinnard started walkin' around the garage and rummagin' through shit. He returned with cans of gasoline. "We gotta torch this place. Get rid of the evidence."

I was all messed up and couldn't even think clearly. "I think we should bounce, maybe call the police."

"What you been smokin'? We ain't callin' no damn police. And what you be tellin' the police? 'Uh, we came here and witnessed this murder?' We be labeled as snitches! We need to destroy as much evidence as possible – like we wasn't even here!"

I nodded, tryin' to think. "Okay, we could call from a pay phone, you know, be anonymous and shit. Chico deserves at least that."

"When the last time yo ass seen a pay phone? And what about Three-piece? His ass gonna hunt us down until we dead like Chico. We ain't got no choice."

Kinnard doused three-piece in gasoline while my stomach churned. I felt sick. "I, I don't believe we doin' this shit, Kinnard. I can't."

"What the hell you got that gun for? Ain't it for killin'?"

"It's for protection. I don't know if I could really pull the trigger." And that was about as honest that I'd ever been with anybody 'bout why I had a gun.

He ignored me. "That's the stupidest shit I ever heard. Now help out."

I was frozen in place and Kinnard came at me hard with breath that smelled like homeless ass. "Look, you have to do this! There ain't no other way 'round it. We gettin' rid of the evidence and him wit' it. Then we gonna go out the same door you came in and split up. Got it?"

I backed up a bit. "Okay, okay! Lemme think." I stood there blinkin', like I was thinkin' 'bout an alternative but the only thing I could think of was landin' back in jail.

He stood there starin' at me. "Lemme ask you somethin'. You sure Chico's dead?"

"You wanna see for yourself?"

"Then it ain't nothin' to think about. If we let this dude live, we will surely be next. Now grab the other gas can and get busy!"

I knew he was right, but as mad as I was at Three-piece killin' Chico, burnin' him alive was a whole 'nother thing. I reluctantly joined in saturatin' the garage with gasoline, but I couldn't put nothin' on Three-piece.

After a while, I stopped and walked over to the roadster. Damn, it was a fine car. Kinnard was readin' my mind.

"I know what you thinkin'. Is there a way to keep this ride and still get your due? You know the answer: hell no!"

I sighed, not wantin' to just concede. "Well, maybe we could…"

"Ain't no way. We don't know nobody that'd take it off our hands who we could trust. Chico was our only connect. You know ridin' around with that would be like puttin' a target on our backs. Ya feel me? All this shit needs to disappear."

There were a few times that Kinnard actually made sense and this was one of them. I knew we couldn't take it with us but it hurt me to my core to torch it.

"Okay. You right for a change."

"I'm always right. You just don't be listenin'." He laughed a little and returned to the task at hand. I wanted to remind him about the car lot mess he got us into, and a host of other missteps 'cause of him, but it was not the time, as Kinnard was known for his selective memory.

When he was satisfied, Kinnard took a bunch of papers and stacked them up near the front door. We both reeked of gasoline. Just then, the assassin's phone started ringin'. Three-piece moaned, his face now swollen to a pulp.

Kinnard said, "You go on out the back and I'll finish this. Get goin' and don't look back."

For some reason, I started to question how much I really knew him. He was too damn calm and once again, we was messin' with fire.

"Where we gonna meet up at?"

"My spot. Now get the hell outta here."

I headed toward the back door, then I stopped. I was rememberin' some valuable details from me hidin' in Chico's closet and listenin' to that fateful conversation.

"First, I gotta check out Three-piece's ride. He got somethin' that belongs to me."

CHAPTER 23

I waited and waited for Kinnard. He lived with Ms. Lena, his elderly grandmother, only ten minutes from Chico's. We've known each other for years. She'd let me in and went upstairs to her bedroom to rest for the evenin'.

I wanted to call him but didn't. I had practically used up all Lena's hand soap tryin' to wash that smell of gasoline off me. I stared at myself in the bathroom mirror; I looked like hell. I didn't even feel like myself. I'd never killed anyone in my life.

Can't say that no more.

I tried to sit and flip through TV channels, but I couldn't concentrate on anythin'. Every siren I heard run through the neighborhood, one after another, had me freaked out. I burned a hole in the carpet lookin' through the window for Kinnard. I checked my cell phone as one hour turned into two.

I wondered if he got arrested. Or did his ass burn up? The thought of it all made me nauseous, and I threw up in the bathroom. I prayed to God to make this all go away, but I knew He wasn't listenin'. My life was proof of that.

I sat down. I stood up. I raided the fridge and downed two Coronas. Then a third and that made my ass chill out for a moment.

Thirty minutes later, he came through the door lookin' like he fell through a chimney.

CHAPTER 24

I jumped up. "Where you been? I was freakin' out!"

He whispered with his finger to his lips. "Yo, calm down. You'll wake Gramma. I know she sleepin." He closed the door and peeked out the large bay window in the living room covered with vertical blinds that used to be white but now they were beige.

Kinnard looked up and down the street. I did the same. It was like we were watchin' a tennis match, but the players were invisible.

Kinnard was different and it was unsettlin'. "Kinnard, is everything a'ight? Why the hell we glued to this window?"

"You know, just makin' sure I covered my tracks." He was talkin' all mysterious 'n shit, but that comment almost made my heart almost fall outta my chest.

"You think you may have been followed?"

"Ant, that ain't what I said. Calm down. We good."

His eyes were wide like saucers. "You know Ant? It was crazy. But right before I threw that match, I thought about Chico. You know, Chico's stash."

"What the hell you talkin' 'bout?"

"Didn't you know Chico was dealin'?" He stayed at the window in observation mode.

"Didn't I say somethin' like that earlier? I didn't know everythin' that fool was doin'. So you knew Chico was into that shit?"

"You could say that. Anyway, I found some-a his stash in his office under the desk in the floor. I just knew he had somethin' hidden up in there, 'cause that's how I'd do shit. Took me like forever to find it too."

Now I understood why he was so delayed. "You saw Chico?"

At first he didn't respond and returned to lookin' out the window. "It was hard not to. It was even harder movin' that dead weight out the way in that fake-ass office chair so I could look for his shit. I need a drink." He walked away to the fridge and grabbed the last Corona.

Then it hit me. "Did you take somethin' you found in Chico's office? You actin' strange."

He got a little peeved. "Yeah, I took his shit! I already told you that. Ain't you listenin'?" He downed his beer.

"That's not what I'm askin' you, fool! Did you take some drugs, Kinnard?"

He smiled. "Damn, you is a good detective. Okay, okay, I just took some ecstasy – well I think that's what it was. Chico had sum-a that too. Got me feelin' real nice. You figured that shit out, huh?" He snickered but I was pissed.

I shook my head at Kinnard's gall. "What about Three-piece? He was out that long?"

"Uh, not exactly. But once I bashed his face in a few times with one-a those car batteries, he ain't make no more noise."

"You did what?" I had an ugly visual of Three-piece's disfigured face.

"Look, it's done. Stop worryin'. We gonna be on easy street."

I exhaled wonderin' how this was the worst day ever, next to bein' locked up. "I guess the placed is torched?"

"Hell yeah! Shouldn't be nothin'' left. It didn't take long for the fire trucks to come. I hid between the crowd watchin' it burn. Had to admire our work, you know."

"You stayed in the crowd smellin' and lookin' like that? What the hell's wrong wit you?"

"Calm down. It was only for a few minutes." He plopped down on the sofa, picked up the remote and flipped channels. "We'll probably make the news."

Kinnard hidin' in the crowd was like an elephant hidin' in a suitcase. Everybody knew our asses from 'round the way.

I noticed Kinnard arrived empty handed. "Where's this stash from Chico's? What was it exactly?"

"We gonna make us a lot of money." He smiled. "Chico had like two thousand dollars and some coke and a bag of pills. Street value should earn us some big money. I left it in my grandmother's ride outside before I came in. I didn't wanna bring no drugs in here. But that ain't all."

"What?"

"Three-piece had a money clip tucked inside his suit

jacket. I counted that shit. It was sixteen hun'erd." He reached down in his shirt and tossed it to me.

The only thing I sold on occasion was weed, well what me and my girl didn't smoke up. I thought about the whole thing and every inch of my gut was sayin' one thing: "Dump it, Kinnard, dump that coke." I handed him back the dead man's blood-stained money clip.

He twisted up his face. "You crazy! I ain't dumpin' shit."

I tried to talk some sense into him. "Listen to me. Three-piece was an assassin. It was a hit! Chico did somethin' to piss those people off. Now you have their shit. We ain't no real drug dealers, Kinnard."

Kinnard spoke firmly, his voice on edge. "Listen to ya dumb ass, just like you wanted to call five-oh. We ain't no drug dealers? But we arsonists. And we murderers. Yo hands ain't clean."

His words sliced me like razor, but I tried to talk some sense into him. "Kinnard, listen to me. We need to leave this alone and lay low. It's a bad idea. I say get rid of it before you end up dead too."

We were both standin', as if about to spar. He wasn't high no more. "Hold on pard'ner. I'm a grown-ass man. If you don't want nothin' to do wit it, I understand. But I ain't dumpin' shit and don't ask me again! And where is that bag of cash at?"

I tried to ignore his question.

He folded his arms across his chest. "Oh, what you

think, I ain't see you? I saw you all in that dude's car, and you did not leave without your own prize!"

I should've known that Kinnard was watchin' me like a hawk. While standin' in that funky closet, I distinctly heard Three-piece tell Chico he was payin' an immediate visit to the Alvarez brothers to pay them off for their tip. My hunch paid off that he had the cash with him. In the back seat on the floor of his ride was a small paper bag. I peeked inside and saw hundred dollar bills. At least it was somethin', and I felt it was rightfully mine.

I got in his face, which reeked of fumes and funk. "Look, I bust my ass to get that car and didn't get one dime for it! I don't know how much it is. I got here and threw it in the hall closet. You forget, I walked back here and left you with my ride. I didn't want to count it with your granny lurkin' around."

"Okay, okay, so what's my cut?"

I was filled with dread. "Really dude? What should your cut be?"

He confidently said, "Half."

CHAPTER 25

We were in the front room, sort of straddlin' the boundary of the living room and the hallway. The staircase was right by the front door and Ms. Lena's bedroom was at the top of the stairs.

If it wasn't for that, me and Kinnard would have been scrapin'. Right now, I wanted to deck him right in his face!

Why's everybody tryin' to screw me outta my money? Can a brotha get a break?

"What the hell kinda calculations you doin' Kinnard?" I couldn't believe the emotion in my voice, and I was strugglin' not to sound pathetic.

Kinnard was annoyed. "I really gotta break this down for you? Okay, I'm the one who took care-a Three-piece. I'm sure crashin' that battery on his head killed his ass. Then I burned the place, which was my idea. I also got Chico's stash, which is like icin' on the cake. Did that explain it for you?"

It didn't really 'cause the only reason we got anythin' was because I stole the car. No car, no money! Again, I was gettin' jerked by my so-called homies. I needed this to be done so I could get outta there. "This shit is whack! Let's square up so I can go the hell home."

He clapped and rubbed his hands together. "Now you talkin'."

"You sure Ms. Lena is sleep?"

"Trust me. Before she lay down, she takes a couple swigs of bourbon. She's out for the night."

I removed the bag from the hall closet, and we went to his grandmother's dining room table.

Before I could react, he grabbed the bag and dumped the cash out. My plan was to discreetly count out his share and just shove the rest back in the bag. Twenty stacks of banded bills tumbled out on the table.

It was the most money either one of us had ever seen at one time. For a few seconds, we just drank it all in.

"We rich! Ha, ha!" Kinnard said like we'd hit the lotto. "Let's count this shit up!"

I couldn't bring myself to crack a smile. My feelings were all over the place.

We started tallyin' up the money. All in all, it was a lousy thirty grand. Chico was sold out for cheap! I was flippin' out over Kinnard takin' charge of *my money* and splittin' the cash between us.

I watched him with venom in my veins. I practically spat at him. "I busted my ass gettin' that car. It was worth six figures. We can't split this! Hell, you got your drugs and cash. I can't do this!"

He was eerily calm. "Just a few minutes ago, you said I'd get half."

I jumped up yellin', "Are you a retard? Have you lost ya fuckin' mind?"

He put his fingers to his lips, "Shhh, stop yellin' up in here! I'm way deep in this shit, deeper than you." He shook his head. "I earned this money. And you know how I feel 'bout people callin' me a retard."

He slid over another five grand. "Here, you weak punk-ass sissy."

"You know what Kinnard? I'm done wit ya ass. You got that?"

"Whatever! You say that lame shit every time somethin' don't go your way. Get over it."

"I'm serious Kinnard. Stay away from me and outta my hood."

JERILYN

CHAPTER 26

Sunday was uneventful. Every Sunday I planned to go to church and then found something else to occupy my time. Like Carmella, part of me was traumatized by our grandparents' forced religion. I wanted these kids to have a spiritual foundation, but I had my own hurdles to get over first.

Monday morning arrived and I stood in the closet wondering what maids wore to work these days. I put on some black slacks and a white blouse and very little makeup. I looked worn out and tired and couldn't stop thinking about how the only one interested in me at the club was gramps. I shook my head, wallowing in my low self-esteem.

I dropped off the kids and made sure to be at the job site at 8:30 AM to wait for my ride. I was instructed to stand near a newly erected statue that held the scales of justice right outside of the building where the public relations firm was located.

When the car service pulled up, a black Lincoln Town Car with lightly tinted windows, I was appalled to see a black man get out of the car. He was average looking, about five-ten, late-fifties, with a small potbelly and a low salt and pepper haircut. He had on casual clothes.

He grinned. "You Ms. Jerilyn?"

I blew out a long sigh. "Yeah, that's me."

"I'm Berkley Patterson." We shook hands. "People call me Berk." He held the backseat door open for me.

I snapped at him, "You don't have to do that! I can get my own door."

"Yes ma'am."

I chose to sit in the front seat, shaking my head, while he closed the door and went around to the driver's side.

He got in the car and proceeded to drive. I was clearly agitated. He asked, "Is everything okay, Ms. Jerilyn?"

"Actually, no it's not! I mean I just hoped you'd be a white guy!" I had forgotten to pray over my lips and already my mouth needed to be under arrest.

He blinked a few times then laughed. "Well, that's a first. Sorry to disappoint you."

"I don't see anything funny. You drivin' Miss Daisy and I'm the damn help!"

He got serious. "Hold on there. This is not driving Miss Daisy! And I thought you were Miss Steinway's personal assistant?"

I rolled my eyes and looked out the window. "Whatever. So tell me, how'd you get this gig?"

"Didn't know you were a reporter too. Let's see, I was a limousine driver for ten years. At one point, I thought I was going to have my own fleet, but that went south. I wanted to do something different. I went looking in the paper and saw an ad for a personal driver. I applied and got the job. Been working for Miss Steinway for ten years now."

I shot him a skeptical look. "Ten years?"

"Yes ma'am. Miss Steinway is good people. And I'd drop the attitude if I were you!"

"I don't have an attitude! I'm just sick and tired of us being at the mercy of these white people."

"Look, if you have a problem with white people, I can turn around if you'd like, 'cause Miss Steinway is definitely white; her mama and daddy were white. Her husband was white, too. There's no escaping her whiteness. And ain't no room for an angry black sister with a chip on her shoulder up in the house. Just say the word and I'll head back."

"You mean the *Big House*, don't you?"

He snapped his neck toward me. "You sure you want this job? Ms. Steinway is usually a good judge of character, but we all make mistakes."

I chose to ignore his comment, although I heard him loud and clear. I was blowing it, so I tried to smooth things over.

"I'm sorry. I'm curious, that's all. I just want to know what I'm working with. Do you drive Ms. Steinway around everywhere, like to work?"

"Actually, I'm on call seven days a week to do whatever she needs. When I need time off, I just tell her. If you must know, she drives her own car quite a bit."

"Am I her first personal assistant?"

"Far as I know, yes you are. She paid a bill twice last month and freaked out about it. Said she needed some help because she was gettin' old. I told her she look damned good for seventy-two. She didn't want to hear it."

"Seventy-two?" I was shocked she was that old. I thought she was much younger.

"Yeah, she takes care of herself. Does a lot of yoga."

I went silent. I watched the neighborhood change from middle-America to upper class society. After a few turns, we pulled up to a structure in the middle of the road. It reminded me of a giant dollhouse, except an older uniformed white guy lived inside. Berk rolled down the window and greeted a man named Lester at the security checkpoint, which he breezed through.

I found out later that it was manned from seven in the morning until six in the evening. Lester Hall had been the guard on duty for several years. If he wasn't at the booth, a security arm blocked your entrance and you needed a code to get in.

House after house looked like something on the front of *Architectural Digest*. Finally, we pulled up in front of an all brick estate and stopped.

Berk announced, "We're here. Normally I would open the door for you, but I don't think you'd appreciate it."

That made me feel bad. "Again, Berkley, I'm sorry. It's been a rough couple of weeks."

He mumbled, "You look like it too."

I was about to reply when I looked up and saw a tall, lanky teen with light skin and sandy colored wavy hair that hung past her shoulders. She was pretty from a distance.

I asked, "Who's that?"

"That is Cherie, Miss Steinway's fourteen-year-old granddaughter. That's my heart!"

My mouth hung open.

He said, "Uh, I need you to get out because you're in her seat."

I opened the door, stepped out and couldn't help but stare at the pretty girl, busy texting on her cell phone. She was clearly interracial with the greenest eyes I'd ever seen.

She took a break to talk to Berk, who was now leaning against the trunk on the passenger side.

"Berk!" She gave him a hug. "I thought you forgot about me."

"Never in a million years." He opened the door for her.

"I told you not to do that." Then she turned her attention to me. "Are you Grammy's personal assistant?"

All I could do was nod.

"Welcome aboard! C'mon Berk, I don't want to be late. You know how Susie gets when we're late. Bye Miss… uh, what's your name again?"

I found my voice, "Jerilyn."

"That's pretty. Bye Miss Jerilyn."

I stood there as they drove off, leaving me feeling like the biggest fool that God made.

CHAPTER 27

Long after the car disappeared out of sight, I remained at the curb wondering what was wrong with me. The day had started off shitty, and I had no one to blame but myself.

I wasn't a racist person; I never really had anything against white people until my mother was arrested. Of course, we didn't have money for a high-powered attorney so we ended up with a white public defender, Mr. Radcliff. As far as I was concerned, he didn't do anything to assist my mother.

Lucille was used to carrying a gun in her purse. She was mugged at knifepoint one evening and vowed not to be violated like that again. She said she would shoot first and ask questions later!

The day she killed her husband, my daddy, she was already very suspicious of his frequent super early *business* meetings. My father, Jonathan Bateman, worked as a help desk computer technician for a healthcare company. She followed him and was heartbroken when he pulled up in front of a hotel. After that, she could not remember walking into the hotel or how she got to his room.

In the room, my father was "gettin' busy" with Dianna Shoreham, a white woman he worked with who also was married…to another black man. No one knows how long my mother stood there watching her husband making love to someone else. Jonathan was her first love, the man she gave her virginity to, put through school and she was also a faithful helpmate! This man had played her for a fool.

According to dad's lover, when they saw her, Jonathan jumped up and started crying, "Oh my God," and "Let me explain" repeatedly. Within seconds and without saying one word, my mother emptied the gun into my father, then turned it on the woman.

The police arrived and found my mother sitting in the corner staring blankly and unresponsive. She was in catatonic shock. When she did become coherent, she wailed uncontrollably saying *someone* had killed her husband.

My mother was an educated woman. She graduated high school and went to trade school to do medical billing. She had a good job, and she thought she had a good marriage.

She just snapped. She had a moment of insanity and Radcliff refused to argue that defense. Several times, Radcliff used stereotypical references…He tried to say my mother was from a typical broken home, with a single parent and she was a product of her environment. Of course she'd resort to violence to solve her problems. That's what they do in the "hood". Matter-fact, he refused to take any advice, citing several times he was the attorney and knew what was best. He constantly told us, "You people this and you people that."

Going to trial with this attorney would surely get her the death penalty. We knew plenty of people who did worse and got less time.

My mother ended up accepting a plea deal for twenty years with no option for parole. He said it was a good deal, since she never had a police record and not even a speeding ticket. In hindsight, this was what the attorney wanted anyway. Less work for his sorry ass. My mother was due to get out soon.

So between that jacked up attorney and that white woman my father had on the side, that nailed the coffin on white people for me for a long time. A part of me knew I was wrong to feel that way but I couldn't help it.

I slowly walked down the manicured pathway to the oversized double front doors. I rang the bell and Ms. Steinway greeted me at the door.

CHAPTER 28

"Jerilyn, welcome. I was wondering what was taking you so long. I gather you were getting used to your surroundings, yes?"

I nodded, "Yes ma'am. Quite beautiful." I stood in the expansive foyer, with inlaid marble tile and a huge, fresh flower arrangement, which set on a pedestal in the center.

"Well, you won't be working outside. That's for Enrique to do, my landscaper. He takes care of all of that. Now come on and follow me to the office."

I did as instructed, taking in the beautifully decorated home. Very traditional with modern flair. After the foyer, hardwood floors blanketed the home, along with impressive crown molding and various types of artwork on the walls.

We passed an extensive library, a sunroom, a living room, a den, a gourmet kitchen and then another room with the door closed and finally, we reached the office, which looked like a cyclone hit it.

"This," and she waved around the room, "is *our* office. I know it looks terrible and as you see, I don't have time to straighten it out."

She walked around the room and pointed at different piles. "I need all of these things filed away; I need to know which bills haven't been paid. I have several unopened pieces of mail. Please sort those according to some sort of system I can manage. I also have a folder here for you to read about my habits and routines.

"There is a box of office supplies here. If you need something more, Berk can take you. There is also a shopping list. Berk knows which stores to take you to as well."

She handed me a pouch. "In here are two one hundred dollar gift cards. Just put the receipts in here so I can keep track of the balance. Any questions?"

"Is there a housekeeper and a cook?" I needed to make sure I wasn't the only other indentured servant.

"Actually, yes, Tatina comes in once a week to clean. I've had three cooks. I'm sorry, but they can't touch my recipes, so I do my own cooking or I just eat out. More questions?"

I was curious. "Are you married? Do Cherie's parents live here too?"

I'd hit a nerve. She became very somber. "I'm not sure what this inquisition has to do with the job so here goes: My husband died eight years ago. He was a very successful investment banker but he loved his work first and it took its toll. This house and the land was already part of his family tree. I just inherited it, not that I didn't have my own money.

"My only child, Stephanie, went away to college one person and came back totally different. She got herself mixed up with the wrong crowd, which led to drug addiction and then she got pregnant. Guess it was my tight grip I had on her. I just thought I was being protective… guess I had smothered the life out of her and she went and found another.

"She had the baby and said she didn't know who the father was. Steffie stayed clean during her pregnancy but soon after, spiraled downward. I did everything I could to save her but when Cherie was five years old, she died of an overdose. That locked room we passed by was hers. Never go in there or else you'll be dismissed immediately."

I just absorbed everything she said, each word one after the next piercing my soul.

I said, "I'm sorry," but somehow it came out like I didn't mean it. And I really did.

"Don't be! It doesn't end there. The daddy showed up when Cherie was seven. He was a very nice looking black man – with HIV. He was in college with Stephanie and he explained how they were all immature and reckless, although he did manage to graduate and clean himself up.

"But the reason for his visit was that he was tracking down all of his past girlfriends so they could be tested. One thing led to another and we did a paternity test. He turned out to be Cherie's father."

Wow, I thought, but this time remained quiet.

"He was as shocked as the rest of us. Cherie spends the month of July and August with him and his wife and son, and also Christmas break. We have a good arrangement, but I have custody of Cherie, trying not to make the same mistakes twice. Now, are there any more questions?"

"No ma'am." After she said all of that, I didn't want to ask another thing. I needed to keep my mouth shut!

"Good. Come, I'll take you on a quick tour of the upper level and then I must get to the office."

CHAPTER 29

Before she left, she had me sign a confidentiality agreement regarding her finances and personal effects. I also signed an agreement regarding being paid seven hundred dollars every Friday. That put a smile on my face. Finally, it looked like I might get ahead. One of the first things I planned on doing was paying off that damn T-Bone from the club. He and my sister had planned another date.

Soon I was alone. I had plenty to keep me busy with straightening out her office. Berk returned and he and I headed to the store for her groceries and my extra office supplies.

We had a relatively quiet ride. I decided I had pried enough into these people's lives. It was a job, nothing more, nothing less.

On the way back, he struck up a conversation. "So, how's it going on your first day?"

"Not bad. So far, it's good." I looked at him sincerely. "I do want to apologize for my behavior earlier."

He smiled. "Apology accepted. You'll see, Ms. Steinway is cool." I got out of the car and he followed me in with the packages.

He showed me where to put her kitchen items and even helped. We chatted about nothing in particular, and I started to feel more comfortable.

He put the last item away. "I'm going to my room and relax."

"Your room?" I sure didn't expect that. "You live here too?"

"Yes, I live in the guest house out back – me and my girl Wanda. Maybe I'll invite you up sometime."

"I see." I had more questions about Wanda, but I had promised myself earlier to try and mind my own business.

He asked, "By the way, did Evelyn, I mean Ms. Steinway, show you *Freddy*?"

"Who is Freddy?"

"Freddy is the state-of-the-art integrated intercom, alarm, music system and a whole lot more. I needed training just to understand this thing. I'll show you what I think you should know."

We stood near the panel while he demonstrated. "There is an intercom system in all of the main rooms in this house and in the bathrooms. They all work the same way.

"I'm Number Three. It rings right to my home. If you need me, just call." He showed me how to do it. He then passed me a business card.

"This is my cell phone. You should probably store this number somewhere."

I nodded.

"This panel controls the lights, the blinds, the heat and A/C – it really is a lot. I'll let her know I showed you some of the features and if she wants me to train you any further, I will."

"Okay. I got some of it." A few of the buttons had pictures on them. I pointed to those. "So I guess this one with the flame is the fire department?"

"Yes, you got it." We went through the other symbols, including the one to dial the police.

"If you press this police symbol, they will come. But there is also a silent signal you can send to the police. Hold down these two buttons." He demonstrated and I paid close attention.

"You'll probably never need any of these, but you never know."

"What if we lose electricity? Will this thing still work?"

"Good question. Yes, we have backup generators that will keep us going for five days."

"What about the alarm for the house?"

"That is confidential information. Only Ms. Steinway can give that out."

CHAPTER 30

The day went by fast. Before I knew it, it was time for me to go home. I had made a dent in Ms. Steinway's office but needed more time to get it in tip-top shape. Berk was ready at 4:30 sharp.

The moment we left the property, his cell phone rang. It was Cherie. He answered, hands free through his earpiece Bluetooth, "Hello, Berk here....Yes, I know you have cheerleading... Susie needs a ride again? Okay, no problem.... Ice cream? Before dinner? I don't know about that....Yes, okay. See you soon."

I smiled at him. "You and Cherie really get along."

"Yeah, she is like the grandchild I never had. She's a good girl. She's an excellent student, does cheerleading and dance, plays the piano, and is studying French and Spanish. She wants to work overseas helping poor people; well that's today's story – you know kids change their mind like the wind. You got kids and a husband?"

"Yeah, three – a set of twin girls and a boy. I have to pick them up by six. I hope this bus is on time! I don't have a husband but I got two baby-daddies. One is a fool."

"They say good men are hard to find. I say it depends on where you look. So where do you live?"

I flatly replied, "In the hood."

"Which one?"

"Franklin Heights."

"Shoot, there are worse hoods! My boy, Peanut, lives out there. He's a driver too – one of those new taxi type deals where you use your own car. Makes a pretty good penny too."

"You mean Uber?"

"Something like that. Hey, I can take you home. I don't mind, but don't tell Ms. Steinway."

"Wow, thanks. After the way I behaved, I can't blame you if you didn't want to do a damn thing for me."

"Well I can only imagine what the soles of your shoes look like. Maybe one day you'll share."

"Yeah, maybe one day I will."

• • •

During my time working for Ms. Steinway, Berk dropped me at home every night. I had no idea what a costly mistake that would turn out to be.

ANTOINE

CHAPTER 31

This was my week to have my son, DeMarcus, and they were on their way here right now. The boy really needed his own room. This pull-out sofa wasn't really cuttin' it but that's the best I could do.

I was really hopin' to have moved into that condo rental, which was a rent to own situation, but the owner screwed me outta the deal, givin' me back half my deposit. That was some jacked up shit to pull, but I didn't have a way to fight it. Said I took too long to come up with the balance and it was in the contract. Yeah…in tiny print that you could only see with a magnifyin' glass.

I finished my joint and cracked open a window. I had incense burnin' to kill the smell.

I was smokin' a lot lately tryin' to erase that shit me and Kinnard went through. But it stayed on my mind day and night, messin' up my sleep. I burned my clothes from that day. Wish I could-a burned the memory up with it. Kinnard was a fuck-up, and I should-a left his ass alone long ago. Now this stupid nigga was tryin' to set up shop with those drugs he found. He was tryin' to buy more with his cut of the cash but nobody was sellin' to him and asked me did I have any ideas. I told him for the hundredth time to leave me outta that shit.

I set up DeMarcus' Playstation and a few new games I bought him. I lined up the two new pair of Air Jordan's and had his entire summer wardrobe laid out on the kitchen table. New shorts and jeans were matched up with new tops; two summer jackets; swim trunks and underwear. A couple-a new baseball caps and some shades. If nothin' else, my son was gonna look fly every day.

Elise appeared in the doorway of our bedroom, naked. "Antoine, come here and give me some lovin'. It's been so long. C'mon over here."

She was so thin, it was unattractive to me. Her tits drooped downward and there wasn't any ass to grab – teeth the color of used teabags. Just skin 'n bones. The thought of touchin' her was the last thing on my mind. We hadn't done it in months. She was rubbin' herself, I guess tryin' to get me up.

Elise stayed high and drunk. I met her at a club where she was a hostess. We had an immediate physical attraction. She had a nice weave that hung straight down her back, complemented by a nice ass and big tits. I didn't mind the weave; kept things interestin'. I couldn't get with no girl whose hair was shorter than mine, and I kept mine close to the scalp. That just wasn't me.

She used to be pretty, with that milk chocolate cocoa skin. Then we had sex, and the head was off the hook. I liked a girl who was about somethin', somebody with some stability. She also kept our home clean and every now and then, she cooked. She could really burn in the kitchen.

At the time, Elise was in night school to do nails; she talked about gettin' her own shop 'n shit. I was into it. We'd lay in the bed and talk about our dreams. Probably could use her place as a front to do some other things too. She was down with that. But all that shit was just that. A bad dream.

I should-a known it was all too good to be true, just like that damn Jerilyn. Her ass thought she was hot shit! I thought she was gonna be my ride or die chick, but she kept pressin' me to get a *real* job. Hell, she had one. Wasn't that e'nuf? So I came up with a plan to start a car dealership and she was diggin' it. That shit was perfect till Kinnard fucked it up! Soon as shit got dicey, Jerilyn jumped ship. Wouldn't even be a character witness for me in court. Then she tried to hide my kid from me. At the time, I had eyes and ears on the streets everywhere. She wasn't keepin' my son from me to raise him like some sissy.

I saw Elise still standin' there, leanin' against the wall. I didn't want none-a that! "No thanks. Why don't you go take a shower? DeMarcus will be here soon."

"Again?" She stumbled toward me shakin' her finger. "You know somethin' is wrong wit dat boy."

That made me mad. "Ain't nothin'' wrong with him! Stop sayin' that shit and get in the damn shower!"

"Why can't he stay wid his mama, huh? We ain't got 'nuff room."

I got loud, "You right! Space is tight. Yo ass is the one that needs to go. You settin' a bad example for him, drunk and high all the damn time! I'm 'bout sick of yo ass! Matter-fact, just pack ya shit and get the fuck out!"

That always shut her up. But one day, I was gonna mean that shit!

"Fuck you Antoine." She stumbled the other way and slammed the bathroom door.

CHAPTER 32

When she got out the shower, she got dressed and looked a little decent, but she was mad and stayed in the back. Good. I was glued to a Jackie Chan karate flick on my new high def TV.

Rapid knockin' at the door could only mean DeMarcus had arrived. I knew Jerilyn had him at some special camp all outta my way that I had to get him to. I couldn't say shit 'cause it was free. I didn't think he belonged there but I couldn't pass up *free*. One day, me and him would bounce *undetected* from this shithole.

"Hey, my man!" Me and DeMarcus gave each other a fist pound. He came in while Jerilyn stood in the doorway. He noticed the new video games and made a beeline to his Playstation.

"These for me?" He was cheesin' hard.

"You know it."

"Thanks Dad! Oh snap!" He noticed his new wardrobe. "Those my new sneakers? Thas where it's at!"

"Yep, got you all ready for the summer too. Check it out." I pointed to my feet so he could see we had matchin' kicks – that aqua blue and black with a white stripe. These was a limited edition.

"Thanks Dad!" He looked through all of his clothes and then returned to his games.

"I'm-a play these right now." He tore into the packaging of the racing game.

I was not expectin' to see Jerilyn still in the doorway. Normally, she bolted. She actually looked kinda cute, with her wavy locks and tight jeans. Anything looked better than that thing I had in the bedroom.

"What 'up Jerilyn?" I subconsciously licked my lips.

"Nothing new. Can I come in?"

That was unusual. "You never wanna come in, but okay." I stepped aside and she walked in, lookin' around as if doin' an inspection.

"Is my place up to your standards inspector?" I asked all white-like with an attitude.

She ignored my question. "Where's those boys at – Elise's kids?"

"Locked up in juvi."

"No way! What happened?"

"What you wanna know for? You gonna bail 'em out? Ain't ya business."

As she walked by, I got a whiff of her perfume and it smelled good. She looked through DeMarcus' summer gear.

He held up his footwear. "Look Mom, me and Dad have the same sneakers!"

"These are all very nice." She picked up a few of the items. "I can take these when I leave, if that's okay."

"Yep. You know I always look out for my son." I wanted to kiss her but I knew she wouldn't let me.

"Is Elise here? Can I talk to her a minute?"

"Elise?" I lit up a cigarette. "Since when you and her kick-it?"

"It's girl talk. She here?"

Damn, her ass was poppin' in dem jeans. She was thick but in a nice way. She always kept herself together – that I couldn't deny. We had a really good thing goin'. If she wasn't so high on herself, we coulda worked somethin' out.

"Girl talk, really? You know she don't like you like that."

"Antoine, please. I just need a few minutes of her time. And I thought we agreed you wouldn't smoke around DeMarcus."

"I'll go get her but she may not wanna talk to you."

I put the cig out and went to our bedroom. Elise was nappin' on our unmade bed. I popped her bony ass. "Yo! Jerilyn said she wanna talk to you."

She squinted at me. "What? Why?"

"Hell if I know. She said *girl talk*."

"Shit, I'm tired. Tell her to go away." And she turned to her side and curled up in a ball. I headed back to the front. Jerilyn was intensely watchin' our son play his racin' game.

Old feelings started to rise up in me. I just wasn't man e'nuf to admit I still had somethin' for her. I rolled up a little closer to her and she saw me comin' and took a little step back, maintainin' her distance, but I stepped in her space anyway, hopin' she ain't see my bulge.

She had her hands on her hips. "Is she coming out?"

I was rememberin' what it was like to kiss her and how it felt to be inside her. I swallowed hard. "She's asleep. Maybe next time."

"Can I go and talk to her?"

I wanted to tongue her down. I couldn't even explain why I had this sudden urge to rip her clothes off. It was clear she wasn't even thinkin' 'bout me.

"What's so damn important?"

"Okay, if you must know, I think my cycle came on unexpectedly and I need to know if she can lend me a tampon or a pad. You happy now?"

That was an instant turn-off. "Damn, okay, I'll go get her." *Women* I mumbled to myself, marchin' back into our bedroom, still wishin' I could replace her with the winch I was currently stuck with.

"Elise," I shouted, "take ya ass to the front. She needs a tampon or somethin'."

Elise shot out the bed with her nostrils flared.

"I ain't the damn drugstore! Shit!" She went in the bathroom, rumblin' through the cabinet. I told Jerilyn she was comin'.

JERILYN

CHAPTER 33

I ran in the back, knowing that my time was short because Antoine was nosy as hell and would soon do what he could to ease his way into our conversation. She saw me and before she could say anything I closed us up in the bathroom.

"Bitch, what you doin'?" Her back was up like she wanted to fight.

I wasted no time, ignoring her insult. "Stop talking so loud and listen to me! I was at the jazz club and saw you in there all over some nigga." I quickly showed her my cellphone shots.

I spoke rapidly, "If I show these to Antoine, he'll kick ya ass all up and down this block and then you'll be a homeless slut. Is that what you want?"

If she was a snake, she would-a bit me. Her eyes were on fire. "You fuckin' bitch!"

"Fine, have it your way!" I went to leave and she grabbed my arm.

"What the hell you want from me?" She folded her arms, still mean mugging me.

I pulled out a plastic baggie. I spoke just above a whisper. "This is DeMarcus' medicine. Give him one pill a day, crushed up in his favorite drink. Don't let him or his father see you doin' it, but he needs this medicine every day every time he comes over here. You understand me?"

She hesitated. "If I get caught doin' this, I'll be in some serious shit."

"You already in serious shit. Just don't get caught! You know he needs this medication. I don't have time to argue with you. You in or not?"

She snatched the baggie. "I don't have a choice, do I?"

"We all have choices Elise. Trust me, you'll love DeMarcus if you keep up his regimen. And you know what else?"

"What!?"

"You need to get yourself cleaned up. You used to be pretty."

CHAPTER 34

I left Antoine's place feeling victorious. I just wish he still didn't look so damn good! I could-a sworn he was checkin' me out and it had been so long since I had a man, I was kinda checkin' him out too, but I could never forget or forgive how he played me and the grief he put me through. But still, a booty call sounded appealing, but I had to first find me a real man!

• • •

After working for Ms. Steinway for a little over a month, I couldn't imagine a better job. I had her office in excellent shape. And she really did need somebody to keep her straight. She had overpaid several bills – some even paid off. I had to call and get refunds on those. She was enrolled in a few mail order prescription plans but had over-ordered. I got that back on track. She was a member on several boards and associations; many of the appointments were either missed or she had put them in the calendar on the wrong date. I had a stack of RSVPs for her to respond to and a bunch of unclaimed dry cleaning tickets, and the list went on and on.

Berk was a good guy. I went and had lunch with him one day at his place and met Wanda. I cracked up when I found out that Wanda was an eight-year-old German shepherd mix he got from the pound when she was just a year old. Berk told me she was his surefire security system and he had trained her himself. At first sight, she growled at me, but on my second visit, I bought her some doggie treats and now we were friends. But there was no doubt in my mind that she would bite the shit out of me if she felt the least bit threatened.

Cherie was actually a nice kid. I expected her to be a spoiled brat but she was anything but. She was just a typical teenager who lived on her phone and tablet. Of course, she was generally preoccupied, but I had to admit she was a pleasure to be around – when I did see her. She was really busy and Berk was fiercely protective of her and treated her just like his own flesh and blood.

And DeMarcus was a different child. Elise was holding up to her end of the bargain. Even DeMarcus remarked how much better his visit was with his dad. I believe as he matured, he'd recognize the importance of his medication, but for now, it'd stay my little secret. Dumb-ass Antoine was oblivious to our scheme and proudly noted that he could see his son getting better, which proved his point that he didn't need to take shit. Yeah, okay. I let him have his fantasy.

I was still collecting unemployment while Ms. Steinway paid me off the books. I was planning on saving for a used car and shared that with Berk. His brother, Frank, liked fixing up cars and had a used Mercedes he was currently working on.

I told him a Mercedes in my neighborhood wouldn't last a week.

He said maybe I was focused on the wrong goal. Maybe I should change my environment first. Right now my rent was subsidized by the government. Moving up would cost a lot more money, but he had a point. Getting my kids to a nice neighborhood with better schools would be great.

And I sure would like to drive me a Mercedes.

Ms. Steinway had said in six months we'd evaluate our working relationship. Now I really hoped she'd make it permanent.

ANTOINE

CHAPTER 35

It had been about six weeks and my funds were gettin' low. I picked up some additional hours at the liquor store, but that wasn't enough money to support me and my son, and never mind Elise. Bitch was goin' through cash like my ass farted twenty-dollar bills. I was 'bout tired of her. Soon we were gonna have a serious talk.

The sun went down while I was waitin' for Kinnard at the park. Said he had to talk with me and it was important. He didn't sound too good. I'd been keepin' my distance from him. Right now, I needed him to come on 'cause the park lights were shot out every other week and this wasn't no place to stand around after dark.

He eventually rolled up in his grandmother's old Dodge Caravan and blew his horn for me to get in.

"What 'up Kinnard?" He was a bit sweaty, with fresh cornrows, and his shirt was stained up with God knows what. I tried to snap in the seatbelt. That shit was broke.

I noticed the windows were all the way down; we hadn't drove a block and I was already suffocatin'. "Do the A/C work in this thing?" I fooled around with the knobs and vents.

"Naw. Been out for a while. I was gonna fix it but it ain't been a priority. We gotta a big problem and this A/C's the last thing on my mind."

"Really? What the hell you talkin' about 'we'? I ain't seen you in forever."

"You know I been branchin' out on my own, makin' my own moves and shit." He wiped his nose and kept lookin' in his rear view mirror, drivin' erratically. "I been sellin' weed and that crack we found. Been doin' really well, but I found this in my mailbox this mornin'."

He dug down in his pants pocket and passed me a note. It read: *"We know you stole our shit. We want it back with interest or else you can kiss your sorry ass goodbye!"*

"Oh shit." I shook my head. "What you gonna do?"

"What am I gonna do?" No, nigga, what are *we* gonna do! We in this shit together man! We was both at that garage, Antoine. We gotta figure a way outta this."

CHAPTER 36

I wanted to go buck wild in the car and fuck him up, but since he was drivin', I ain't want him to crash us up.

"Pull over Kinnard. Pull the fuck over!"

He pulled into a supermarket shoppin' center and shut the engine off.

His right leg was bouncin'. "After I got this note, I received a phone call. I don't know how they knew my number…I couldn't even talk! They told me I had three days to get fifty thousand dollars, and I needed to close up shop right now, today. Said when they called again, I betta have that money."

I was breathin' heavy because it was hot and the more he talked, the more furious I was.

He kept on talkin'. "I have 'bout fifteen. What you got left from the garage hit?"

I turned my head toward him, speechless. I didn't even know if I believed this bullshit story.

"Look, Kinnard. I told ya ass to leave that shit alone! I told you I ain't want nothin' to do with it. I made that fuckin' clear, Kinnard. This ain't my problem, dawg! This is your fuckin' problem. Count me out!"

He calmly said, "They mentioned you too."

I blinked a couple of times while my heart skipped a few beats. "What the hell did you just say?"

"I said they know 'bout you, *dawg*! So you go ahead and get out if you wanna. But they gonna come gunnin' for you when they don't get what they want from me."

"How the fuck is this happenin'? I ain't been on no damn streets sellin' they shit! How Kinnard?"

"I told 'em me and my homeboy would get their cash and everything would be a'ight."

I banged the dashboard. "Why you pull me into this shit, Kinnard? Why?"

He looked genuinely hurt. "Man, I thought we were boys. We known each other forever. I should-a listened to you, I should-a left they shit alone, but I didn't. I'm sorry." And he sat there and cried.

I almost joined him 'cause I didn't know how we was gonna get fifty thousand dollars and keep on livin'.

CHAPTER 37

After he got himself together, he said, "I think your girl got it." He wiped his nose with some KFC napkins.

I sat there tryin' to rub my headache away. "What girl? Elise don't have shit. Her car is even at the junkyard."

He shook his head, "Naw, not Elise. Jerilyn."

I almost laughed. "You crazy? Where you get that idea from?"

"Every day, she leave out lookin' nice in the mornin'. Every night, she come back in a black sedan, like a car service. Drops her 'n the kids right in front the buildin'."

I was intrigued. "You serious? A car service 'n shit?"

"Yeah. I was curious, ya know." He paused. "Now don't get mad, but I followed her yesterday."

"Go on."

"She got picked up in Farragut Square and they drove out to Courtland Gardens. I got the license plate. The house where they went, it had like a security check. I drove up to the window and acted like I was a delivery man but the old dude had shit locked down. He said my name wasn't on the list. I mentioned Jerilyn's name, and he said he had to call her and check. I told him let me handle it. I pretended to call her and reschedule our hook-up. Yo, these are some million dollar homes."

I was silent for a number of reasons. DeMarcus mentioned his mom was workin' but I didn't think nothin'' of it. I figured she was tempin' somewhere. She did that from time to time. But this was a whole different ballgame.

"Anyway, I left and parked outta sight. I hung around all day. A few times, I pretended I was broke down and had my hood up, you know, to throw shit off. 'Round four, she and that black sedan came rollin' out.

"We only got three days Ant, three days. We could hit this place and I know we'd be straight. You got a better plan?"

CHAPTER 38

I sat there not knowin' what to say or feel. And what kinda job was Jerilyn workin' way out there? She ain't tell me shit about this new gig. But that'd explain why she was lookin' good these days. But robbin' a house? That ain't me.

"Look Kinnard, we gotta think of somethin' else. Besides, we don't even know what house! You didn't really see it, did you?"

"Do I hafta think of everything?" He forced open the glove box and gave me a greasy slip of paper. "Let Jo-Jo verify that plate number. Hell, maybe he can even get the money for us, you know, crack into that bank account; ya feel me?"

I looked outside away from Kinnard, as my blood pressure rose to the point that my ears were burning.

I knew Jo-Jo because of Chico. We had only met two or three times at Chico's shop. With Chico outta the picture, word on the street was Jo-Jo was laying low. His place had been raided by the police. They didn't find shit but it let him know they were watchin' his ass.

"Why you so quiet, Ant?"

"Really Kinnard? You done dug us a hole so deep, I can see the gates of hell. I'm not down with this at all." I blinked back tears of anguish. "Wish I never stole that ride. Wish Chico was still here. And right now, wish I never let you into that garage."

He cut his eyes at me. "I get the feelin' you don't have my back, Antoine. That ain't a good feelin'. If it wasn't for me, we'd probably be dead right now. I'm the one who took care-a that problem named Three-piece, 'member? I put myself on the line for you, *my brotha*! Did I ask to be dragged into that shit? You text me to help you out. I had yo back! You owe me!

"And you concerned wit that girl Jerilyn? What the hell she done for you, Ant? She always thought she was better 'n you. You ain't nothin' to her but a hoodrat."

I rubbed my eyes together as the poundin' in my head tried to take over my vision. "Okay, okay. Gimme a day to think on somethin' else."

"Have… you… been… listenin'… to… me? That's one thing we ain't got. Time."

He started up the van and it caught on the third try. We drove in silence and ended up back at the park.

"Yo Kinnard, can you take me home? It's only a few more blocks."

He stared straight ahead as if it hurt to look at me. "Naw, I can't."

I exhaled. "Look, I know you upset. Let me just have one day to think on it. Gimme twenty-four hours. I'll call you tomorrow. We good?"

"Can you get the fuck out?"

I bounced and barely closed the door before he sped off. I headed home, my mind spinnin' in a million different directions tryin' to decide what we should do.

I knew I had about seven grand at home; that meant we were short by a whole lot. Much as me and Jerilyn didn't get along, I just couldn't picture myself breakin' into her new gig for possibly nothin'. Kinnard's plan, as usual, was royally fucked up!

I turned the corner and my face smacked the pavement. They were on me, kickin' and punchin'. I counted at least three dudes. They was jackin' me up so bad, I couldn't even react. I didn't even have my piece on me. I did my best to fight back, but one bad-ass against three bigger bad-asses was no match. After a couple more blows to the face, I was KO'd.

CHAPTER 39

Don't know how long I was out but I woke up in a chair. My hands were tied behind my back and my ankles were strapped to the chair legs. My head was explodin'.

I was tryin' to remember what the hell happened when a bucket of ice cold water hit me in the face. That shit stung like an ice-packed snowball. My lip felt swollen and my face hurt. A high beam light blinded me.

"Listen up, Antoine, and pay close attention. You and your boy in some serious shit."

I tried to focus on the distant voice. Sounded like a white dude.

"We know Chico had some of our drugs stashed in his garage. We also know that one of our own ended up dead and was set on fire in that same garage. But he was a contract hire trying to prove himself. If that was not the case, if he was family, you and Kinnard would be in little pieces all over the city right about now.

"You know, I got my own spies. All of a sudden your buddy Kinnard is selling more than weed. He's selling crack! Now where the hell did he get that crack from?

"I checked around and nobody sold it to him, you know why? 'Cause people know the rules, Antoine. There's rules to this game and if you don't play 'em right, you get burned, no pun intended. I also found out he was around at the time of fire, standing in the crowd. A pretty dumb move, if you ask me."

He paused and I was sittin' there thinkin' I was a dead man. My insides felt like loose jelly. I wanted to plead for my life and beg for another chance; I wanted to tell them I'd give them anything and I'd do anything not to die, but I didn't think it would do no good.

"Antoine, word on the street is you frequented that garage too. Apparently you like jackin' cars and you pulled off a beauty. Shame it never got delivered, but that's neither here nor there right now.

"I told Kinnard I needed fifty thou; now I need a hundred. I thought about it. I can't let y'all off so easy or else it'll get back to the wrong people. You got three days. But I need every cent. In cash! If not, one day your son don't come home. Then your girl gets sliced up and gang raped, and your sister might lose a limb. And what happens to you last will be slow and very painful, I promise. Shit happens all the time. You understand?"

My voice cracked when I spoke. "Please don't hurt my son. I'll get you the money."

"Good. I think you have a lot more sense than your friend. When I was talking to him, he seemed a bit off."

I closed my eyes, wincing in pain. "Okay, uh, how will I get in touch with you?"

"Good question. I will come to you at midnight three days from now. We know how to find you. Now in a few minutes, we're gonna untie you. Then about three minutes later, a timer is going to go off and a light will come on. At that point you can leave, but not a moment sooner. We clear?"

"Crystal."

"Good. Oh, and when you leave, take out the trash next to you."

CHAPTER 40

In the dim light, two masked beasts untied me. From where I was sittin' they looked about six-feet-five of pure muscle. Then the flood light was switched off and the room went practically dark. I could hear rumblin' 'round; a door opened and closed. Then nothin'.

I sat there paralyzed with fear. I wondered how long it had been. I couldn't move. I could barely think. Every nerve in my body was on edge. I tapped my foot on the floor waitin' for what felt like fifteen minutes; then an overhead light popped on, and I had to shield my eyes with my hands.

I blinked several times to adjust my eyesight. It appeared I was in some sort of condemned buildin'. I looked to my right to find Kinnard next to me. He was also tied to a chair and his head hung limp. He looked dead.

"Kinnard!" I screamed his name and fell straight to the floor tryin' to get over to him. The circulation in my limbs was just wakin' up, and it was painful. I got to my feet then backed up when I saw his face. He was beaten so badly, I barely recognized him. I put my ear to his bloodstained chest. He was still alive. I untied him.

I shook him gently, "Kinnard, wake up, please." But he was totally unconscious. I hooked him around me and dragged him outside the abandoned buildin'. I couldn't make out where we were, maybe Maryland. With my aching body, I could barely hold his weight, so I eased him down to the ground.

Instinctively, I checked my pockets. My wallet and cell phone were still on me. That scared me. I was sure they'd scrolled through all my contacts and now they knew everyone I did and in some cases, had their addresses. I called for an ambulance.

• • •

The Prince Georges County Maryland hospital said Kinnard had two cracked ribs, a concussion, a broken jaw and was in a coma. They stitched up my face and treated my wounds then sent my uninsured ass home. I told them we were the victims of gang violence and they bought it. Wanted to know if I wanna file a police report. I said *For what?* I couldn't ID nobody.

I made it home on mass transit. Elise was out cold. I got in the shower and the tears flowed like a river.

I did not sleep that night. Every little house noise had me reachin' for my gun. I stayed on the couch thinkin' about Kinnard and how I had to tell his grandmother we *was mugged.*

I watched the sunrise and went over my options for the hundredth time – the same fuckin' options from the previous night.

After using the facilities, I stayed in the bathroom and smoked a joint, examinin' my battle scars. Face was so bruised, parts of it was black. There were two fist size bruises on my chest that hurt to the touch.

I closed my eyes tightly, shakin' my head tryin' to wish it all away but when I opened them, not a damn thing had changed.

Elise came in the bathroom naked; she grinned and said, "Thought I smelled breakfast." She took a hit then tilted her head to the side and looked at me as if for the first time.

"Damn baby." She gently stroked my face. "What happened? Who did that to you?"

"I had a fucked up night." I inhaled, held it, let it out slow.

"Anythin' you wanna talk 'bout?" She kissed each of my nipples.

"Naw, just a lil' scuffle."

She ran her fingers over my chest. "Who looks worse, you or him?"

"Kinnard looks worst." Another hit passed between the two of us.

She giggled, feelin' nice. "Kinnard? You 'n him fightin' like you was kids?"

I didn't want to answer, so I didn't. She kissed my lips softly, then my cheeks and then nibbled on my ear, and I imagined she was someone else. She started playin' with her own nipples gettin' them erect.

"Lemme make it all feel better." She slid down my boxer shorts and dropped to her knees. I let her do her thing and for a few minutes, everything was all right. For a little while, I forgot that if I didn't get that 100K, I was a walking dead man.

When she was done, she got in the shower and invited me to join her. I declined. I had a phone call to make.

Jo-Jo answered on the first ring. "Wat-up?"

"Yo, my man. This is Antoine."

"Who?"

"Antoine, you know, Chico's boy who got that roadster, 'member? We met once or twice."

It was quiet. Then, "The fuck you want?"

I wasn't quite sure how to take his hostility. "Need a favor."

Long pause. I could tell he was thinkin' hard 'bout tellin' me *go fuck yo-self*. But he said, "See you 'round three at the bowlin' alley," and hung up.

CHAPTER 41

'Nother damn humid day; I already needed a second shower, thanks to the overcrowded bus. I stood outside Mack's Bowling Alley a little hesitant to go in. Jo-Jo didn't sound too friendly but still, he agreed to meet with me. I mean me 'n him didn't have no beef, so really, this should be a simple transaction. Even tho he was raided, I knew he hadda way to keep the cash flowin'.

There was always 'nother way to do dirty work.

I went inside the outdated facility. Mack's was well known in the community, someplace we all used to come back in the day for some bowlin' fun. There used to be video game tournaments, bowlin' leagues, card games (Spades, Bid Whist), and birthday parties. The owner, Philip Mackey, used to keep it up real nice. Once he invested a shit load of money – had it lookin' somethin' like Dave and Buster's. Mack forgot he was still in the hood. After several heartbreakin' break-ins, he just did the bare minimum to keep it operational, and he never tried again to modernize the place. He paid off the buildin' durin' the time of plenty, so now it was just somethin' to do, since he was widowed with no kids.

The current crowd was mostly old dudes who were retired with time on their hands playin' dominoes or checkers; and occasionally, some adults would bowl. Every now and then, a group of kids wandered in but they didn't stay too long. Mack was old-school, close to seventy, and he refused to play rap music or what he called *studio tricks*. He'd say, "Dat girl only sound like dat 'cause-a dem usin' studio tricks."

We couldn't convince him otherwise, like we couldn't convince him to see a dentist. He said they was just quacks and losin' teeth was natural. Yeah, he had a funny way about him but a big heart. Durin' Christmas, he always had a toy drive, and he would also sponsor some of the little league sports teams in the area.

The only reason the place still had a steady stream of customers was the café.

Ms. Olanda Spates and two-a her cousins ran the eatery, "Mack's Big Cheeze." They had awesome baked goods and the food did not disappoint, like seafood gumbo, chicken corn chowder and split pea soup along with one of their signature sandwiches. They kept their daily menu small and pretty much the same, so everythin' was good all the time and it was reasonably priced.

Sunday brunch was the crowd pleaser. You could get a Sunday fried chicken dinner for just ten bucks, along with their famous macaroni and cheese. So thanks to Olanda, they stayed in bid'ness. Probably pick up somethin' on the way out.

I strained to see if Jo-Jo had arrived and the dim lightin' didn't help, along with my shades to hide my scarred face. I moved to the back of the room, while Al Green sang *Love and Happiness* in the background. I saw Jo-Jo seated at a table next to a brother I didn't know with a patch over his eye.

Jo-Jo was a big dude, 'bout five-eight, four hundred pounds. Almost his whole body was tatted up, except his face, with ships, pirates and mermaids. His thick hair was neatly cornrowed back into a ponytail under a Washington Wizard's basketball cap. His black t-shirt read, "Two Tons of Fun". He didn't look like he had missed any meals, so I knew he was not hurtin' for cash.

"Hey Jo-Jo, wat up?" I went to give him a pound, but he did not return the gesture. He stayed seated. I imagined draggin' his big ass up and down had to be a chore for him. I chose to ignore him not givin' me some dap, even tho that was disrespectful. He didn't even introduce me to his boy. I grabbed an empty chair and pulled it up to the table.

He took off his cap then put it back on. "You know what? I almost didn't hook up wit you. Word on the street is that you torched Chico's place. You do that shit?"

Damn, that caught me off guard with a jab below the belt. I tried to hide my guilt with added distress in my voice. "C'mon, you serious right now? Hell naw. I'm still tow-up behind that shit." I was a bit shaken that people were doin' that much talkin' on the street, and the Russos probably contributed to the noise.

He folded his hands on the table. "They didn't have no money to bury him properly. You know that? His ass is in an unmarked grave."

I never even thought about Chico's funeral or anything of the sort. I just figured he was burnt to a crisp. "Wow, that's fucked up. I mean it seems like the fire would-a been somethin' like a cremation."

"You got jokes, huh? That shit ain't funny, and that ain't what I heard. He was fount back in his office with a bullet to da head." He motioned his hand like a gun and pulled his trigger finger pointed at me.

My insides were loose and I fought to hold it together. "Who said that shit? I didn't see nothin' in the papers 'bout that."

He jumped all over me. "The papers?" He looked at me skeptically. "You sayin' thas how you get yo news, bruh? Nigga, pleeze! But I tell you this, Antoine. My experience is the streets don't lie. It don't matter much now. Police ain't goin' t'do nothin' about us killin' each other. But you don't know nothin' about Chico dyin', right? I mean you jacked that car – *everybody* know 'bout that. But then that car never made it outta the garage. Bet you ain't read that in no papers."

I was nervous and my heart was knockin' against my chest. I wanted to just leave 'cause it was obvious Jo-Jo was piecin' some shit together, and I was right in the middle of it. But I had nowhere else to turn, so my ass stayed seated.

I kept my voice steady. "All I know is I dropped the car off as scheduled. Afta that, I bounced."

"So you say!"

A fine, brown-skinned Latina with long wavy hair came over with two bowls of gumbo for Jo-Jo and his friend, along with two fat grilled cheese sandwiches and two glasses of sweet tea. It looked and smelled good, but right now the thought of eatin' made me nauseous.

He flirted with the girl. "Damn you fine, you know that?"

She just smiled and returned to the counter, and we all watched her ass as she walked away.

"This is some good-ass food!" After a few slurps of his tea, Jo-Jo reclined back and said, "Hey, ain't you 'n Kinnard boys? That nigga been runnin' 'round here all of a sudden like he's a dealer or sumthin'. You know the Russo's don't play dat shit."

I asked him, "What you know 'bout the Russo's?"

Jo-Jo looked at his pard'ner. "Tell 'em."

When he spoke, I could see nothing but gold fronts. "Back in the day, the Russo family used-ta control *all* the action on the streets but as the old heads died off, less and less new blood was interested in stayin' in the game. Da few thas left control what comes in and outta here and who can do what."

Jo-Jo jumped in. "Okay, story time is over! Back to my question. What you know 'bout Kinnard dealin'? I know the Russo's ain't put his retarded ass on the payroll."

I got heated. "What the fuck I know 'bout Kinnard? I ain't with him 24/7." I knew Kinnard shouldn't have stayed in the damn crowd. I knew him taking those drugs was a bad idea. "We beefin' right now anyway, and I ain't seen him!"

He and his friend exchanged glances. Jo-Jo tapped the table with his spoon. "Why's that?"

I shot back at him. "Why's what? I came to ask you for some info. Not play this game-a twenty questions. Is you snitchin' for five-oh or somethin'? Damn!" Even tho I may have been on my way to gettin' a second beat down, I had to let him know I wasn't no punk.

"Am I five-oh?" He sat straight up and scowled at me. "Did you jes axe me that? I should have my baby bro here put a cap in yo ass!"

It was then I saw they actually did resemble each other, except his baby bro was fit and looked like a damn brick wall. He lifted his shirt to show me his gun.

Jo-Jo took a bite of his sandwich. "You know Chico was my dawg. Me 'n him, see, we was in high school together. Back then, I was a lightweight. I know, hard t'believe right? One day, these boys jumped me. The reason why don't matter, but the only one who even thought about helpin' me was Chico. We was friends since then.

"We had his'try. But you...I only know you 'cause-a him. Then you call me up on the phone – what kinda dumb shit is that? You know these fools is listenin'. I know you heard what happened. So, what the fuck you want, Antoine?"

I wrestled my emotions back in check, swallowed hard, and passed him the piece of paper from Kinnard.

"This is a license plate number. All I wanna know is this person's 411, and if they's connected to anyone in Courtland Gardens. I need whatever you can find."

He looked down at the paper then picked it up and pocketed it. "I need five hundred."

I reached inside my shirt and pulled out an envelope containing seven hundred. I laid it on the table. "Here's seven for your troubles, but I need it like today. That possible?"

His brother checked the envelope; told Jo-Jo, "It's legit."

He pointed his chubby finger at me. "What I'm-a need you to do is get a burner phone. Send me the number. I'll text you the info all septic like."

I raised an eyebrow and his brother clarified, "He mean cryptic like."

Jo-Jo twisted his neck toward his bro then back at me. "Ain't that what I said? Anyway, destroy the phone afterwards. Can you handle that?"

"Yeah, cool."

"I mean if I call that phone later and someone answers, thas gonna be another ass whuppin' for you."

I jerked a bit. "What?"

"Dem shades ain't hidin' what you think, Antoine. But let's be clear. Thas all I'm-a get you is information. I'm not doin' no transactions. I'll contact you t'nite and don't axe me for another thing, 'cause I don't like you. Understand?"

CHAPTER 42

I made my way back to the apartment, where Elise was knocked out on the couch. An empty bottle of Hennessey was sideways on the end table. I just shook my head.

I hadn't eaten all day. After that meetin' with Jo-Jo, I wanted to roll outta there as fast as possible. Waitin' to hear from him was gruelin', so I kept myself occupied with video games, karate movies and eventually, I ordered a pizza. Elise got up and wanted to hang out and talk 'bout our future together. Women pick the damndest times to talk about shit. I never told her what really happened. Wouldn't have made a difference, but actin' like we was in love was the last thing on my mind. I wasn't in the mood for none-a that, so she got mad and stormed out. I was glad she was gone so I could think.

Several hours later, Jo-Jo texted over the information in bits and pieces. I had to use a pen and paper to figure out what the hell he was sayin'.

The owner of the car was Berkley Patterson. He lived in Courtland Gardens and was also employed by a Ms. Steinbeck, who was a rich bitch. Her late husband had money, too.

Jo-Jo included a link to an article 'bout the Steinbeck woman's husband in a magazine called, *Money Talks*. Most of it was borin', but then a few things were interestin', like how he had a gold coin collection.

But who keeps things like that just layin' 'round the house? All of that shit was not liquid. True, Jerilyn had definitely moved up, but Kinnard was gamblin' it would be an easy mark for some quick cash.

The more I thought about it, the shadier the plan became. There had to be another way! After I made a few notes, I destroyed the phone. It was well afta two in the mornin' before I could convince myself to get some sleep.

• • •

At six in the mornin', I woke up screamin'. My t-shirt and boxers were stuck to me like plaster. I dreamed I was back in that abandoned buildin' with Kinnard. I swung my legs over to the side of the bed with my head in my hands tryin' to see how I was gonna live past tomorrow. I looked over to Elise's side of the bed, but it was empty. She hadn't been back home.

That freaked me out. The Russos had threatened me and my family; now Elise was gone. She never stayed out all night! I checked my phone for a message, but there was none. I called her number, and it went to voicemail. I texted her: *Where you?* No response.

They said I had three days, but I didn't trust them worth a damn. I paced and called her again. Voicemail. I started talkin' to myself then my phone chimed with a text message. It was her: *At my sis house for a few days.*

I replied, *When u be back?*

After a super long pause, I texted the question again. She said, *IDK.*

I let it alone. Maybe she was gone for good, but I wanted to be the one to leave her ass. I was sure she'd be back. Her holy-roller sister didn't mess with drugs and alcohol. Yeah, Elise would be back.

In the meantime, I had one more play to make but it was worse than eatin' crow, rather it was like eatin' crow's shit!

I made another phone call and disconnected it before it went through. Shit!

I put the call through again. Jerilyn answered quickly.

"It's me, Antoine."

"Yeah, I know who it is. It's early. What's up?"

"Look, I'm in a serious life or death situation. Believe me, I wouldn't call you, but I don't have nobody else to call. I need your help real bad."

I hesitated. "I need a loan for ninety thousand dollars."

The phone went dead. I called her back, cussin' her out till she answered.

"Jerilyn, please don't hang up. Listen to me."

"Antoine, if you askin' me for money, the answer is no all day long."

"Okay, I know I burned you in the past. I didn't mean it. I have apologized over and over again. Please. This time, I'm in serious trouble. People are threatenin' to kill me, Jerilyn. Please."

The phone was silent but she was still there. Then she said, "I can't help you with that kind of cash."

"Ain't you workin' now?"

"So what? You think I'm makin' six figures? Think again! I got maybe three hundred dollars saved."

"What about a loan? Can you get a loan?"

"Goodbye Antoine."

"They gonna kill me, Jerilyn. Please. You know I wouldn't call you for no shit like this unless I didn't have a choice. Kinnard's in the hospital in a coma. I'm in some bad shit. Please." It hurt me to my core that I was beggin'.

"Hospital? Who did he piss off? And why don't you call your attorney sister, Antoine? I can't do it."

"We not talkin' right now, okay." I wished I could call my sister, but I owed her two thousand from three years ago, and she was fed up with me not payin' her back time after time. It wasn't that I never had the money. I just never got around to it. She blocked my number and went totally AWOL on me. I didn't even know how to find her.

I was walkin' 'round in circles from the stress of the situation. I had to go deep to get her attention. I used the only ace in the hole. "What about DeMarcus?"

She paused. "What about him?"

"These people, they threatened to kill *everybody*. I need to pay them this money or our son could be in danger. They'll kill him, Jerilyn!"

"How could you stoop so low as to use your son to get out of your jacked up situation? You know what? I don't believe you. Don't call again!" She hung up.

Kinnard was right. She didn't give a shit about me.

She left me no choice.

JERILYN

CHAPTER 43

Me and Berk had a rhythm going now. In the mornings, we'd treat each other to breakfast. He wasn't a big coffee drinker until I introduced him to flavored coffees and now he was hooked. After riding together for seven weeks just about every day, I found out a lot more about him and his life, and I opened up about mine as well. It felt good to have someone older to talk to who had a different perspective on things. He was really helping to keep me grounded.

The Steinway household went to church regularly, including Berk. Ms. Steinway was Methodist and Berk went to a nondenominational Christian church. One day, he invited me and the kids. He knew my religious background but he said if I came once and didn't like it, I wouldn't have to come back. So one Sunday, he picked us up.

That first day, we actually enjoyed ourselves. The children went to classes designed just for them, and when the pastor started preaching, it was if he was talking about me and my circumstances.

That day, there was an altar call for prayer. I ran to the front with a crowd of other people. I received the Lord again in my life and when I did, I felt such a burden lifted. I stood there crying and praising God for all He'd done for me. In spite of every wrong thing I did in my life, God still loved me. It was a revelation and redemption at the same time.

I had a long way to go to be what I considered a good Christian, especially keepin' my lips in check, but that was okay. We were all works in progress on the Master Potter's wheel. Being in church made me feel complete. I joined the church on the spot.

It was the beginning of August and shaped up to be a muggy day. I'd gone shopping for a decent wardrobe and for the first time in a long time, I felt good about myself when I stepped out the door. Those thoughts of being Ms. Steinway's hired help were long gone. From day one, she had shown me nothing but love, respect and kindness. God was at work even then, and I was reminded while in church how I prayed for a job and He certainly delivered. At the time, I was just too stubborn to see it or receive it.

It was Friday and tonight, me and Carmella were going back to the jazz club to check out Porter's band. I was looking forward to just having a good time.

Carmella and T-Bone were still dating. He was going to meet us there later. I was cool with that. I actually invited Berk, but he hadn't confirmed he was coming yet.

I stood by the scales of justice and waited for my ride. I had a treat for Berk. A chocolate cookie crumble Frappuccino.

It was overpriced but you only live once.

He pulled up on time. Dag, he hadn't been late once. Today, my hands were full. Ms. Steinway wanted me to attend a fundraiser with her and it was a formal affair. She said in the future, I'd probably attend other events in her place. I was open for that.

She gave me a five hundred dollar gift card to buy two dresses, and I was showing them to her today. I had the garment bag in my hand, my purse on my arm, and the crate holding me and Berk's coffee drinks. I did a balancing act and opened the car door.

"Good morning Berk."

"Should I get out and help?" He laughed, and I joined him, both of us, no doubt, remembering the first day we met.

I confidently replied, "I got this." I passed him the garment bag, which he placed in the back.

I smiled at him but he looked distracted, as if looking past me. He shouted, "Hey you…"

But it was too late. A masked man with a gun shoved me in the car. I tried to struggle, but it all happened so fast, I couldn't even explain how three of us, me, Berk and the gun, ended up in the front seat.

"You…you can take the car." Berk stuttered, "We'll get out."

The man with the black knit ski mask and oversized grey hoodie hammered back with a deep voice, "You ain't in charge. Start drivin' to the house and turn up the damn air condition."

"Look, son, you don't have to do this," Berk said a bit more composed. "You can have this car. Just let us get out."

I was sandwiched between the two men and did not recall how the expensive coffee was spilled all over my new yellow sundress, the seat and the floor.

The man cocked his gun. "Ain't ya son! Now I'm gonna say it one mo time. Drive to ya house in Courtland Gardens. If you don't do it, I'm gonna shoot this bitch, 'cause I don't really need her. But you I need. We clear?"

Berk glanced at me then nodded. "Okay, okay." He put the car in gear and drove.

I blinked a few times, just to see if I was dreamin', but I wasn't. This was for real. We were being carjacked and kidnapped at the same time. I was now a crime statistic. I prayed someone saw this all going down and called 911, but it happened so fast.

The closer we got to Ms. Steinway's house, the more frightened I became. Cherie was there waiting for Berk to take her to the airport for a month with her father. Ms. Steinway would be waiting for me. My stomach was in knots. I continued praying silently for deliverance from this situation. I prayed for our souls and for wisdom to see a way out.

Berk took the long way, something we did when he knew there was an accident or traffic jam. I surmised he was doing this to stall us getting to the house, like maybe he was trying to think of an 'out' or maybe hoping to flag down some authorities. The air-conditioning had me shivering.

The carjacker barked, "Put some music on in this bitch!"

Berk tapped the radio knob and Dottie People's song, *On Time God* rang out from the gospel station. That totally infuriated him.

He reared back and stomped the radio twice, his knee slamming up against me, bruising parts of my body. The knob for the volume and power were smashed in awkwardly, yet the music continued to play.

And that's when I saw it. I might not have even noticed it, except DeMarcus made such a big deal out of it.

I didn't want to admit I knew who was behind the mask. There were a couple of times I thought I heard his voice quiver, as if disguised, but the sneakers sealed the deal.

It was Antoine for sure.

What the hell was he doing? I reflected back on that phone call he made to me. Somehow he knew I was working for someone with money and now he was gonna try and rob the place.

I closed my eyes, praying the entire time for us to make it out of this alive. My whole body vibrated while stick pins jabbed at my stomach from my nerves being on overdrive.

When we were about ten minutes from arriving, Berk pulled over and slowed the car to a stop. He was trying to do everything in his power to not take this situation to Cherie or his employer. He looked at Antoine. "So what's the plan?"

"Is you crazy? Who told you to stop? Plan is for you to shut the fuck up, drive to the house and get me my gold coins."

Berk's heart was doing a rapid handclap. This man meant to rob Ms. Steinway of the gold coin collection that she kept in a safe deposit box at the bank. He responded, "I see. Okay, so we get you these coins. And then what?"

"You talk too damn much." And he fired the gun.

CHAPTER 44

A canon.

It sounded like a canon exploded in my ear. I don't know what made more noise – the gunshot or my screaming. Antoine cocked the gun at me, then put the butt of it against my cheek.

"Close yo mouth or I'll shut it for you." His anger overtook and practically erased his attempt to hide his identity. I was drawing in short breaths to keep from bawling, but I was on the brink of losing my sanity. I wrapped my hands around my body and rocked back and forth. I didn't know anything about these coins, and I knew we were in deep trouble.

Berk's window was cracked into tiny spider web pieces but almost entirely still in the window frame, except for a hole the size of a quarter in the middle. He'd shielded his face with his arms and he lowered them slowly.

The intruder said, "Next time, I ain't gonna miss. Now listen up. I'm only gonna say this once. Don't talk unless I ask you a question. Now drive to the house."

Berk looked at me and I saw his Adam's apple go up and down and the fear in his eyes. His hands shook around the steering wheel. He started the car, and I saw tears on the verge of sliding down his face.

Berk's phone rang. It was Cherie. He did not answer.

Up ahead was the security booth where Lester was waiting for us. I was hoping he wasn't there because when he wasn't around, the security arm would have been down. Then Berk would have used a code to activate it, but there was also a security code he could have entered as a silent alarm.

"Stop the car!" Antoine wrapped his left arm around my neck; his forearm pressed painfully into the side of my chin. He told Berk, "You find a way to get us through this checkpoint, or I'm gonna shoot her."

Berk raised his hand like in class to ask a question. Antoine yelled, "What?"

"I, I can't lower the window. It'll just shatter. I think it's best if I get out. I'll leave the door open and you can hear everything. Unless you have a better idea."

"No fuckin' way, you ain't gettin' out. Matter-a-fact, don't stop. I'm sure he knows you and this car, don't he?"

Berk kept his tone even. "That isn't procedure."

"Well it is today! Keep drivin'."

CHAPTER 45

Berk floored the pedal, with Lester hanging out the security booth calling his name. Berk's phone rang. It was Lester.

Berk said, "I need to answer this." He picked up Lester's call without waiting for permission.

"This is Lester, Berk, you okay? You practically ran me over."

"Hey Lester, yeah, uh, sorry, but I need to use the bathroom badly. Catch you later." And Berk hung up.

We slowly pulled into the driveway but not in front of the house, where Cherie was standing with her suitcases.

Seeing Cherie sent a jolt threw my body. Antoine was in desperation mode which meant the man I thought I knew was not the same man behind the mask. This was my cross to bear. Cherie nor Mrs. Steinway needed to be involved, and I could not put their lives in further danger. I can't even explain it, but I knew that if we were going to make it, I had to calm down and take control. If this was my last day on earth, no one else needed to join me.

"Who's that?" Antoine snarled.

I said, "She's a guest. She's waiting to go to the airport. She'll miss her flight if Berk doesn't take her."

He jammed his gun into my ribs. "Guess she's gonna miss her flight. Pull up then get the fuck out!"

I knew Berk was in agony. The thought of Antoine coming in contact with Cherie was unthinkable.

Berk pleaded, "Please let me call this young lady a cab and get her as far away from here as possible."

"I told yo ass to shut up!"

Cherie started walking toward the car.

CHAPTER 46

My voice was hoarse as I pleaded with him. "I know you want money…and the coins. We can get it for you. There's a safe hidden in the guest house. Berk can drive us there."

"In the guest house? That shit don't sound right."

I spoke from an unwritten script. "It's in the floor. Like if anyone hits the main house, they would never think of also looking in the guest house. The owner don't believe in keeping everything in one place."

Berk followed my lead, "Yes, that's right."

Antoine sneered. "Fuckin' rich people! Well I need two hundred thou plus those coins. Is that in the safe?"

Berk said, "Way more." He pulled off right before Cherie reached the door. She stood there shouting his name. He drove faster. She called Berk's phone again.

Berk's voice trembled, "Let me answer this. Please."

"Put the shit on speaker." Antoine growled.

"Hello, this is Mr. Berkely."

"Mr. Berkely?" Cherie sounded exasperated. "I know your name! What're you doing? I'm going to miss my flight. We've got to go."

Berk spoke sternly but fast, "I need you to have Ms. Steinway call Freddy. Tell her it's an emergency and I'm sick. I can't take you. Freddy can take you. Bye." And he disconnected the call before she could ask another question. She called back and he did not answer.

We arrived at Berk's house and parked the car. Antoine got out first. "You both get out on the driver's side. You better not be lyin' to me."

Berk got out and I slid over to the driver's side and exited behind him. My neck and side were sore.

I figured Wanda would tear him up as soon as he entered the house, but there was a chance she could get shot first. I didn't see where we had much choice.

I told Berk, "Give him the keys, the combination, and tell him where to find the coins and money."

Antoine hauled off and hit me in the side of my head with the butt of his gun. It caught me off guard and I tripped over my feet. He angrily told me, "You ain't in charge."

Berk approached him cautiously. "Look, you don't have to hit her. We're going to give you what you want."

"You keep on runnin' yo mouth and I'm tired of it. Listen up. We all goin' in together, and you, ol' man, you gonna get me what I came here for. We clear?"

Antoine reached under his hoodie and pulled out a compact nylon bag. He threw it on the ground in front of Berk. He motioned with his gun for Berk to pick it up, which he did. With Berk leading the way and me close behind, we headed in the direction of his home, until I stopped a few feet from the front door.

This was all my fault. I let this fool into my life and now I had put other people in danger. Blood trickled down the side of my face and my vision was blurry, but I had to fight. I could not let Antoine win. I knew in my heart what I had to do to save these people I had grown close to in such a short time. I turned and faced the masked man.

"Antoine, why are you doin' this? Because I wouldn't agree to get you a loan? So you out here robbin' my employer, threatening to kill people and even threatening to kill me? What about your son? Is this how you want him to remember you? In the name of Jesus, stop this now."

He froze a bit. And pulled off his mask.

CHAPTER 47

He waved his gun at Berkley for him to stand next to me. Antoine's face was swollen, bruised and covered in beads of perspiration. It shouldn't have bothered me, but it hurt me to see someone had beaten him like that.

"Oh my God, Antoine. Look at you." I could not stop the tears.

Antoine's countenance was dark and evil. "You think you smart, huh? You always thought you was better 'n me. I tried to keep you outta this, but you wouldn't listen! Kinnard got me in some shit and they said they gonna kill me and DeMarcus and everybody! I'm tryin' to save my son's life! I would-a traded your sorry ass life but you ain't worth shit! Now get me my fuckin' money and those coins!"

He looked like a madman. His eyes were wide and wild, and even his grip on the gun had become unsteady.

I thought about my kids and all they meant to me and how much I loved them. My mother and grandparents flashed through my mind and how my death would affect them if I didn't make it. And my best friend and sister, Carmella. She could be a trip, but I loved her more than life itself.

I didn't want to die. Not like this.

I wrung my hands. "Antoine, this is not the way. You have got to go to the police. I'll go with you."

He pointed the gun at my face. "Oh *now* you wanna help? Get this door open and stop talkin' before I pull the trigger. Understand?"

I slowly nodded, defeated.

Antoine looked around, "Hurry up."

Berk's hands shook as he keyed into the door. He turned his head ever so slightly and caught my eye as if to say *get ready* and then said, "This way."

Berk opened the door and Wanda came to greet us. When he heard Antoine close the door behind us, Berk yelled "ATTACK," then rolled to his right. Berk tried to pull me with him, but I stepped back out of his reach and threw an elbow as hard as I could into Antoine's gut, which surprised him; then I did my best to get out of the way.

It all happened with lightning speed. A couple of bullets went flying as Antoine tried to shoot the dog, but he missed.

Wanda did her job and was all over Antoine. I counted my blessings that Wanda had familiarity with me. She was trained to attack strangers and guns. Antoine's screams pierced the air as the dog continued to maul him.

When Berk was satisfied Antoine was disabled, Berk yelled, "HALT." Wanda got off of Antoine and stood on the alert by Berk's side, who was now holding Antoine's weapon on him.

Somewhere in the midst of the chaos, my body was on fire. Hell of a time to have another hot flash, except this one was different. One side of me was warm and sticky. My right chest area felt like a giant bee sting but the pain was worse than any insect bite.

My dress, that was covered in coffee, now had cherry mixed in except it wasn't cherry. It was blood. My blood.

I was crouched down against the wall and then collapsed sideways. Berk came over to me, but he looked all fuzzy, like in a fog. I was barely conscious, drifting into somewhere peaceful and safe. Even the pain was gone.

Berk gripped my shoulders. "Jerilyn, just hold on."

ANTOINE'S EPILOGUE – 6 MONTHS LATER

CHAPTER 48

I never liked dogs. That "man's best friend" shit I always thought was for white people. I wanted to kill that damn dog, but the bitch was too fast. I woke up many a night relivin' the fuckin' attack. Sometimes, I was yellin' in my sleep. In jail, that shit's not cool.

Half my ear was bitten off and a permanent scar was gouged into my cheek. My gun hand had permanent damage. Nerves and tendons were all fucked up. I couldn't hold a pen or a fork without bein' in pain. When I signed my name, it was scribble. I was in physical therapy, but mostly, I was learnin' how to use my left hand. Shit was hard.

When they told me I shot Jerilyn, I had no reaction, no feelin' 'bout it. It was never my intention to shoot no one. I just wanted the coins and money. And as usual, the path I took was a dead-end. I shoulda known that anythin' Kinnard planned would be a dumbass failure.

I was assigned a public defender, a Mr. Radcliff. I hated his ass from day one. He wanted to take a plea deal. I was charged with everythin' possible – kidnappin', attempted murder, armed robbery, assault, carjackin' and a shitload of other charges created just for black men like me. I told him I wanted to go to trial. He had several fucked-up reasons not to – all bullshit! Said I had a record and didn't stand a chance, so I took the fucked up plea.

Once that crime boss threatened my son, I hadda act! I did what I hadda do and I hoped that one day, I could explain that to DeMarcus. I started several letters but trashed each one. Probably couldn't read my writin' anyway. One day, I'll actually mail one to him.

Kinnard eventually came outta his coma. Said he couldn't remember nothin' after he and I met up at the park. 'Course, he probably had *no memory* of what happened at Chico's neither. No matter what, he 'n I would not snitch on each other. To this day, I don't know if he really couldn't remember or if he indeed had some brain damage. I always thought he was touched anyway.

I was sentenced to twenty years while Kinnard was released to his grandmother's care. Heard he quickly moved outta the neighborhood. Never saw nor heard from him again.

Some nights I dreamed that Kinnard rolled on Russo for a plea deal. How else he get to walk? We was serious about not bein' bitch-ass snitches, but that was before we got our asses kicked. Part-a me wonders if that was a dream or if someone told me that and I just couldn't accept it.

Goin' back to prison was my worst nightmare. At least my latest crime spree had earned me mad props with my new roommates. But sadly it just meant I was where I belonged – behind bars with every nutcase that ever lived. I used to think I was better 'n them, but I was the same. Word on the street was cops busted a good amount of the Russo clan and forced them to close up shop.

Some of them were probably in the same shithole as me. On my bunk the other evenin' was the ace of spades, a playin' card with my name on it. Means I'm marked for death, probably from Russo's people. My daddy sealed my destiny for me. He died here. I'll probably do the same.

I joined a gang for protection, but they always need me to do favors 'n shit – stuff I can't even talk 'bout.

Elise came to see me once. Told me that it was because of her sister that she decided to go into rehab and get herself together, but she didn't offer any other details. She was lookin' sweet too. Then she made it clear that even though she loved me, she wasn't waitin' 'round twenty years. No shit! She left sayin' she'd keep me in prayer. I told her *save ya breath*.

Every religious group tried to recruit and convert me. I wasn't hearin' that noise. I couldn't be saved. Didn't wanna be. It wouldn't get me outta here no sooner.

Still, my cellmate prayed over my soul, left me Bible scriptures and shared with me the goodness of the Lord. If my heart wasn't so hardened against the hand I was dealt, I might've been able to receive what he was sayin'. But I was convinced that in my next life, I'd be just as fucked up as I am now, and I didn't have nobody to blame but myself.

JERILYN'S EPILOGUE

CHAPTER 49

One of Antoine's bullets caught me in the shoulder and exited out the back. I also had a slight concussion. Thank God that was the extent of my injuries.

When I came to, I found Ms. Steinway, Berk and Carmella by my hospital bedside. Carmella cried so hard. I didn't know she had it in her.

Berk filled me in, since I passed out soon after I hit the floor. Turned out that once Cherie told Ms. Steinway Berk's "Freddy" message, she knew right away there was something seriously wrong. Ms. Steinway had not gone into work just yet. She had wanted to see Cheri off to the airport.

She followed up with a call to Lester and after the report she received from him, she didn't waste any time calling the police. Cherie was instructed to stay in her room with the door locked. Ms. Steinway owned a glock, and she sat by the front door until the police arrived with her weapon prepared to fire at any would-be intruders.

The police were exiting their vehicles when gunfire erupted from the guest house. They entered Berk's cottage with guns drawn. Once they saw the situation was under control, they took the gun from Berk and placed Antoine under arrest.

Berk said Antoine looked a bloody mess. He was mumbling incoherently that "they" gonna kill us all, and he just kept repeating it, as if in a trance. No doubt Antoine was headed for serious jail time.

Even though I was expected to be released in a week, the first thing on my mind was my kids and who was gonna take care of them. To my amazement, Carmella said she'd make sure they got to camp and she'd do whatever was needed. When Ms. Cora heard what happened, she offered her services at half price. That made me smile. Gotta admire a compassionate businesswoman.

When Berk and Ms. Steinway had some alone time, Ms. Steinway was not happy when Berk told her he'd been taking me home in the evenings and picking me up for church. It didn't take long to figure out that I was being watched and Antoine somehow put the pieces together.

Ms. Steinway told Berk he was too kind, but she understood why he did it. And then she broke down and cried at the thought of losing not just two employees, but friends, in the same day.

Berk and I grew tired of repeatedly telling our side of the story – to the police and anyone who asked. Mostly, it felt surreal, like there was no way I went through this horror. But I did and lived to see another day.

Even though I was new to the church, I had a steady stream of visitors. They brought flowers and fruit and most of all, their prayers. I didn't have a lick of health insurance. A fundraiser was being held in my honor to help with the medical bills. Ms. Steinway agreed to match whatever funds were raised plus some! I never cried so much as I did during that hospital stay!

My grandparents came up from down south and for the first time in years, my sister treated them with kindness and respect.

It wasn't till weeks later that I reflected on how everything worked together for the good for those who loved the Lord. Seeing my sister and my grandparents getting along made me so happy. They offered to stay and help out, but I declined. Somehow all of us in my place didn't sound too appealing.

Berk was by my side every day. He had a lot of free time on his hands with Cherie gone to be with her dad. Even though we were several years apart, we had a connection, a bond. Sometimes traumatic experiences drive people apart. This brought us closer together.

On the day of my release, my arm was in a sling, but my legs worked fine. Nevertheless, hospital policy stated I had to be placed in a wheelchair. The nurse wheeled me to the curb and the heat of the day warmed my soul. Berk was there waiting. He got out of the car, came around, and opened the front passenger door.

Carmella stepped out looking refreshing in peach colored jeans, and a white halter top with multicolored wedge sandals. Her hair was pulled back into a high ponytail. I smiled at the sight of her, proud to have a foxy sister.

I stood up so the nurse could wheel the chair back to the hospital.

"What're you doing here?" I hugged my sister tightly with my one free arm.

When we separated, she grinned and held my hand. "I wouldn't have missed this day for all the money in the world."

As if on cue, Berk opened the back passenger door.

I should have kept the wheelchair because the sight of her almost knocked me off my feet.

Right in front of me was the best gift ever. My legs could no longer fully support me, as I collapsed into my mother's arms. The three of us – me, my sister and my mom – were wrapped up in each other as what could only be described as unconditional love.

In the midst of my happy tears, I glanced over at Berk who had the biggest grin his face could handle. His eyes glistened as he shared in our joy from a distance.

I mouthed, "Thank you," to him and he winked in return.

At that moment, I was reminded of a line from one of my favorite movies, The Color Purple: *I know'd there is a God.*

Yes, there is!

ABOUT THE AUTHOR: JC GARDNER
www.booksbyjcg.com

Ever since the age of twelve, I aspired to be an author. Writing stories became an escape, a way for my imagination to come alive on the handwritten pages of steno pads, notebooks and journals. A closet writer for many years due to my 7th grade teacher humiliating me in class by calling my book of poems plagiarized, when it came to sharing my writing, a cloud of self-doubt would follow that it wasn't worthy or good enough, so it would stay buried, deep within a drawer, a satchel, or just locked up in my mind. An extrovert by nature, slowly but surely my love of writing seeped into homemade greeting cards, personalized poems for friends, song lyrics and of course, lots of stories. After many years, I've finally been able to embrace my purpose. What God has placed on your heart, no one can take away.

My desire is to inspire others to keep the faith and follow their dreams through writing workshops, women's conferences, and as a writing coach, ghost writer and consultant.

I'm also available as an inspirational speaker to help others release the damage from the past and walk boldly into their destiny. Thank you for your support. Email me: authorjcg@yahoo.com.

More Books From

www.PerfectPublishing.com

070621-100-2-60W